WHY IS MY CHILD IN CHARGE?

WHY IS MY CHILD IN CHARGE?

A Roadmap to End Power Struggles, Increase Cooperation, and Find Joy in Parenting Young Children

CLAIRE LERNER

ROWMAN & LITTLEFIELD
Lanham • Boulder • New York • London

Published by Rowman & Littlefield
An imprint of The Rowman & Littlefield Publishing Group, Inc.
4501 Forbes Boulevard, Suite 200, Lanham, Maryland 20706
www.rowman.com

86-90 Paul Street, London EC2A 4NE, United Kingdom

British Library Cataloguing in Publication Information Available

Library of Congress Cataloging-in-Publication Data

Names: Lerner, Claire, author.
Title: Why is my child in charge? : a roadmap to end power struggles, increase
  cooperation, and find joy in parenting young children / Claire Lerner.
Description: Lanham : R & L, [2021] | Includes bibliographical references
  and index. | Summary: "Through stories of her work with families, the
  author shows parents how making critical mindshifts-seeing their children's
  behaviors through a "new lens"-empowers them to solve their most vexing
  childrearing challenges. Claire Lerner offers a roadmap for implementing
  practical and proven solutions that are based in science and work in real
  life"—Provided by publisher.
Identifiers: LCCN 2021003809 (print) | LCCN 2021003810 (ebook) |
  ISBN 9781538149003 (cloth) | ISBN 9781538192726 (paper) | ISBN
  9781538149010 (epub)
Subjects: LCSH: Child rearing. | Behavior modification. | Parenting. |
  Parent and child.
Classification: LCC HQ769 .L3855 2021 (print) | LCC HQ769 (ebook) |
  DDC 649/.1—dc23
LC record available at https://lccn.loc.gov/2021003809
LC ebook record available at https://lccn.loc.gov/2021003810

For Sam and Jess,
I adore and appreciate you more every day.
You are my inspiration to
never stop learning and growing.

AUTHOR'S NOTE

The stories in this book come directly from my work with families. The names and identifying details have been changed to protect their confidentiality. Some of the children featured in the cases throughout this book have an underlying special need, such as a sensory processing disorder or significant anxiety. Many of the strategies I suggest can be very effective in managing the challenging behaviors these children struggle with. But, if you have a child with special needs, or who has experienced trauma, or whose challenging behaviors are so frequent and intense that they are interfering in her daily functioning, I strongly encourage you to consult with a child development professional with whom you can work directly to make a full assessment and devise a tailored intervention plan.

CONTENTS

ACKNOWLEDGMENTS

There are so many people who helped make this book possible, to whom I am immensely grateful.

To the families I work with, who have allowed me into their hearts, minds, and homes to partner with them to be the best parents they can be. In my world, they are the "perfect" parents: when things with their children aren't going in a positive direction, they take the time to step back to reflect, gain new insights, and make the necessary course corrections to put in place a better path for themselves and their children. These kids are so lucky to have such sensitive moms and dads guiding and supporting them as they grow.

To my agent, Joelle Delbourgo, and editors, Carrie Cantor and Suzanne Staszak-Silva, who believed in the power of these stories to provide meaningful support to families with young children.

To ZERO TO THREE, my professional home for more than twenty years, for providing endless opportunities to build my knowledge and skills alongside the most talented and committed group of early childhood experts and champions.

To Teri Kozlowski, Sami Cook, and Jenny Gorski of Teekoz Kids, my incredibly talented OT colleagues, who helped me understand the powerful role sensory processing plays in understanding what makes children tick, enabling me to significantly enhance my ability to help the parents and children I serve.

To my amazing posse of friends, Marianne and Mark Barabak, Karen and Bob Deans, Barbara Gill, Barbara Albert, Lynette Ciervo, Nancy Shapiro, and Brian Glick. A special shout-out goes to Nicole DeCario, parent of the most feisty and adorable toddler, who read the entire manuscript and provided invaluable guidance on how to make it better; Barbara Miller, master of the meticulous, who took the final look to be sure this manuscript was not submitted with even one typo; Lesli Rotenberg, branding genius, who worked her magic to come up with the perfect title for this book; and who, along with Marisa Nightingale, master media strategist, worked fervently to help me reach a much wider audience.

To my brothers, Stephen Lerner and Alan Lerner, and step-kids, Sammy Bar and Justin Bar, who provided endless encouragement for which I am so grateful.

To my mom, Renee Lerner, my most fervent supporter and eager editor. No one catches a run-on sentence or awkward phraseology like my mom.

To my husband, Rich, whose unconditional support and patience, and unparalleled ability to keep me laughing, even in my most frustrated moments, afforded exactly the relief I needed from the intensity of the book-writing process and got me over the finish line.

To my son, Sam, who helped me learn many of the lessons that are embedded throughout this book, about what highly sensitive children really need from their parents to thrive and the incredible joy they bring with all of their charisma, creativity, and passion.

Last, but not in any way shape or form least, to my daughter and editor extraordinaire, Jess, who read every single word of this book through an insane number of iterations and provided exceptionally incisive and detailed feedback. Jess solved problems that kept me up many nights. And she did it all with the calm and clarity that her highly reactive mother so desperately needed. I truly could not have done this without her.

FOREWORD

Toddlers are a joy and a challenge, all at once. I have worked with young children and families for nearly three decades. I do so with passion and enjoyment knowing that it is a short, yet highly critical, time in a child's life. I can say with certainty that this is the most delightful of ages and also one filled with intense frustration for toddlers as well as their parents. Toddlers are a bundle of contradictions. They can be delicious and demanding, charming and challenging, fun loving and ferocious. Often, these dueling sides of toddlers and young children occur back-to-back or nearly simultaneously, which is why this age can be so perplexing to parents and other caregivers.

When Claire and I first met several years back, we immediately connected over our mutual love of young children and families and seeing how hard it is to be a parent of young children. We discussed how the pressures on parents were growing (and this was long before a pandemic set in). We joined over our desire to support parents during these "tough and tender" years that are toddlerhood.

Fast-forward a few years. I was delighted to learn that Claire was writing this book. In my book, *How Toddlers Thrive*, I took a deep dive into the world of the toddler, but the piece I thought parents could use more of was understanding their own thinking and approaches in the heat of the moment with their children. Claire wrote that book for you.

Based on her work with thousands of parents and their young children, Claire addresses a range of typical toddler dynamics that are emotionally loaded for parents. Through detailed anecdotes of her work with families, Claire helps you see how your mindset matters in how you respond to your child, especially in the most maddening moments. She shows how making some key mindshifts can unlock the door to new and more effective ways of managing these complex situations and provides hands-on tips for addressing these perplexing behaviors. She does so with respect and sensitivity to the needs of the child. This book will take you to a more enjoyable place with your toddler with her straightforward and well-tested advice on how to handle trying situations.

This "early childhood manual" will make possible more joyful moments with your toddler and greater calm for everyone involved. It will empower you to give your child the best start possible. Ready for that? Read on.

Tovah P. Klein, PhD
Author, *How Toddlers Thrive*
Director of Barnard College Center for Toddler Development

INTRODUCTION

I never had any intention of writing a parenting book. There are so many good ones already out there that provide very helpful information and strategies for dealing with the range of child-rearing challenges that arise in the early years. What could I possibly have to add?

Most parents who seek my consultation have already read many of these excellent parenting books. They are well aware that they, not their children, are supposed to be in charge. They know that limits and boundaries are essential for keeping kids safe and secure and to help them learn to cope with life's inevitable frustrations and disappointments. They are clear on the importance of managing their own emotions and not losing it when their child is melting down, but, in the heat of the moment, they get triggered into reactive mode and resort to yelling, bribing, negotiating, and threatening, all of which are tactics they know are ultimately ineffective and potentially detrimental.

The lesson is that reading books by experts is one thing but carrying out their advice when emotions are running high is another. By the time parents arrive in my office, most of them are feeling out of control and helpless. They are berating themselves for being incompetent in the face of a human a third their size and are often frustrated and angry at their children for making them feel this way. They despair that the three to four precious waking hours (at best for working parents) they have with their children are spent in power struggles and negotiations, with lots of aggravation and not enough joy.

So I asked myself, what is the missing piece of the puzzle? What is the obstacle to moms and dads being the parents they want to be?

I found the answer as I carefully observed how the dynamics unfold between parents and children in their most challenging moments in the reality of their homes. I started incorporating home visits into my practice because parents were coming back, consult after consult, reporting that the strategies we had come up with in the comfort of my stress-free office were great in theory but, back home, when confronted with their children making irrational demands, defying a direction, or saying and doing inappropriate things, they were triggered into reactivity mode and had a hard time implementing a "positive parenting" plan.

As I guided parents to reflect on and analyze these maddening encounters with their children, I began to gain insight into the core stumbling block: a number of consistent, parental mindsets that result in moms and dads reacting in ways that are ineffective and often increase the intensity and frequency of meltdowns, power struggles, and other challenging behaviors. For example, the legion of parents who were tearing their hair out and dreading bedtime because their children were making incessant demands for more books, more water, or more cuddling time—essentially more of everything. The routine could go on for hours. Parents were exhausted, angry, and feeling helpless to establish a bedtime with boundaries. When we explored what was keeping them from setting limits at night, the most common culprit was their feeling in these moments that it was mean to say no to something their child said she needed and that the tantrums that would ensue when their child was denied the extra story or bedtime snack were inherently harmful to her.

And, then, there were the parents frustrated by their children's "not listening" or cooperating. These parents had tried everything—multiple reminders (aka nagging), cajoling, rewards (aka bribery), and threats—to get their children to follow a direction. The faulty mindset at play for these parents was that they needed and had the power to control their children—*to make them behave*—and that the way to go about this was by using the above tactics to get their children to change their behavior and comply. The problem is that these strategies were leading to less, not more, cooperation because the outcome of the situation was in their children's hands; it was dependent on whether the child accepted the bribe/reward or feared the threat and agreed, for example, to put down his toy and get into the car seat.

Until these kinds of subconscious beliefs become conscious, they continue to get in the way of parents acting on their best intentions and providing the loving limits, boundaries, and supports their children's need to thrive. Once parents become aware of the mindsets at play in their interactions with their children, they are able to make essential *mindshifts* that make it possible for them to change their reactions to their children in a way that reduces challenging behaviors and creates more positive connections between parents and children, as illustrated in the case of Daniel, Aviva, and Gracie:

> Daniel and Aviva come to see me because they are ensconced in endless power struggles with Gracie, their three-year-old. They are confused and concerned. They have read a lot about the importance of giving children choices and want to help Gracie feel empowered and have a sense of agency, but things are spiraling out of control. "She now thinks she's an equity partner," Daniel explains. They give her a choice about whether she wants mommy or daddy to do bath time. She chooses mommy, but the second Aviva goes to help Gracie into the bath, she insists, "No, daddy do it!" Aviva calls for Daniel, but—shocker—Gracie has changed her mind again and wants mommy. At book time, Gracie will insist that Daniel read to her even when it's mommy's reading night. She will make a huge ruckus and refuse to listen to the book until Aviva throws in the towel and gets Daniel to take over. At breakfast, Gracie asks for toast but insists on a whole new piece because Aviva cut it the wrong way. When Aviva tries to convince Gracie to accept the toast because it's the same piece of bread regardless of how it looks, Gracie tells Aviva that she "doesn't know anything about food" and that she wants daddy to make her toast the "right" way.

Daniel and Aviva are finding themselves exasperated and angry with Gracie much of the time, which saddens them. They have started to think of her as their "little fascist dictator." They know that the dynamic with Gracie is unhealthy, but they feel stuck. They don't know how to get her to accept limits and cope with not getting her way or having things done exactly as she expects.

The first step in our work together is to help Daniel and Aviva take a step back and analyze these encounters with Gracie: What do they think the meaning of Gracie's behavior is? What kind of self-control do they expect from her at this age? What is getting triggered for them when she makes demands they think are unreasonable or she melts down when she doesn't get her way? What stops them from sticking to limits that they believe are healthy and appropriate for her?

Through this process of reflection, Daniel and Aviva gain some important insights that lead to helpful mindshifts, the first of which is that Gracie isn't purposefully trying to drive them crazy or misbehave. She is doing exactly what three-year-olds are driven to do, pursue their goals through whatever means are successful. And further, that her inflexibility—the need to have things done in exactly the way she demands, as irrational as it may be—is a feature of her temperament. Gracie is a highly sensitive little girl whose brain never turns off. She processes and overthinks everything. She gets overwhelmed by the flood of thoughts in her head. To make the world more manageable, she comes up with fixed ideas about how things should be, such as the way her toast needs to be cut or the exact spot where she wants Daniel to park the car when he picks her up from school at the end of the day. When she is overwhelmed, it can lead to very dysregulated behavior, such as the constant changing of her mind. She doesn't know what she wants, so nothing Daniel or Aviva try to do to help satisfies her.

With this insight that Gracie is not being manipulative nor trying to drive them crazy on purpose, Daniel and Aviva change their mindset from "Gracie is a spoiled dictator" to "Gracie is a little girl who is having trouble managing her big emotions and needs our help to learn to cope with important limits and boundaries."

Another mindset at play is that, when Gracie is distressed, Daniel and Aviva feel—at a cellular, gut level—that this emotional state is harmful to her. Daniel, in particular, is worried that Gracie will not feel loved if he says no to reading with her because it's mommy's turn. Daniel's parents were cold and distant. He vowed that he was going to forge a close bond with his children. He doesn't want Gracie to feel rejected by him. This mindset makes it especially hard for Daniel to set appropriate boundaries. What loving parent is going to set a limit if he thinks it will be harmful to his child? But, as we take an objective look at the dynamics during these power struggles, Daniel and Aviva are able to see that, by trying to accommodate all of Gracie's demands, they are creating more distress and discord for everyone and fewer moments of joy and positive connection. In short, their approach is backfiring, resulting in exactly the outcome they are trying to avoid. With this insight, Daniel and Aviva are able to make the mindshift from "It is mean and rejecting to not give Gracie what she wants" to "What Gracie wants is not necessarily what she needs and that the distress she experiences when things don't go her way is not damaging to her." In short, they are able to see that limits are loving.

A third mindset that needs shifting is that Gracie means exactly what she says. This is something Aviva is particularly struggling with because Gracie is going through a "daddy" stage. When Gracie is rejecting toward Aviva, criticizing her or pushing her away, Aviva is responding with hurt and anger, which is creating more tension in their relationship and amplifying Gracie's favoritism toward Daniel. Once Aviva understands that going through these phases doesn't mean a child loves one parent more than the other and that children blurt out all kinds of outrageous and sometimes venomous statements when they are in distress mode, she is able to shift her mindset from "Gracie means exactly what she says" to "Gracie is struggling to manage her complex emotions, and I can't take her mean verbiage and actions at face value."

Making these mindshifts—interpreting Gracie's behavior through a new, corrective lens—enables Daniel and Aviva to make positive changes in how they handle challenging moments with her. They continue to give Gracie choices, but within limits. Accordingly, they decide that it is important for *both of them* to be part of the bedtime routine so they don't give her carte blanche to decide who does bath time and books. The choice they give her is which parent will do bath and which will read books.

As is expected, the first night Daniel and Aviva implement the new plan, Gracie tests it. She chooses Aviva as the book reader but then quickly changes her mind and says she needs daddy. Aviva takes deep, calming breaths and reminds herself that the system she and Daniel have set up is loving, even if Gracie's reaction suggests otherwise. (I think of this as the "positive parenting paradox." Sometimes, what feels mean is actually loving, and what *feels* loving is not always what's most helpful to a child.) This enables Aviva to acknowledge Gracie's demand while sticking to the limit: "I hear that you want daddy to read, but this is a mommy book night. So I am going to continue reading. It's up to you to decide whether you want to listen—that is your choice." Gracie shouts that she will not pay any attention and pronounces, "Mommy, you are a bad reader." She then proceeds to hide under the covers. Aviva reminds herself that Gracie does not mean exactly what she says. She is acting on her feelings in the only way she knows how. Getting reactive will only perpetuate this dynamic. For his part, Daniel, who can hear what is transpiring from down the hallway, resists the strong temptation to go in to resolve the situation by caving to Gracie's demands. Aviva proceeds to read the book with a lot of animation to clearly demonstrate to Gracie that she isn't angry or hurt and that she isn't going to be derailed by Gracie's protests. Once Gracie sees that Aviva is going to stay the course and that daddy isn't coming to read, she stops shouting, slowly emerges from under the blanket, and cuddles up for the remainder of the book.

The shifts in mindset that Daniel and Aviva make are life changing for them and Gracie. This lived experience of providing Gracie the boundaries she so desperately needs but that she has been so fiercely fighting has a powerful, positive, overarching impact. When she is spiraling out of control and can't regulate herself to make a good decision, providing a clear boundary helps her more quickly regroup and get back into control. Now, Aviva and Daniel constantly remind themselves that just because Gracie might not like a rule doesn't mean it's not good for her. This new mindset has enabled them to feel much more comfortable and motivated to set appropriate limits across the board, which has resulted in the whole family experiencing much less stress and more joy.

As you can see from Aviva and Daniel's story, and as you will see from the many stories told in the pages that follow, mindsets can be changed, but first they need to be made conscious. Often, what feels intuitively right and loving is counter to what children need. Making some important mental modifications enables you to more clearly see and address the root cause of your children's behavior. You are able to assess the situation more accurately. You no longer fear the tantrum and are able to stick to essential limits and become more effective and loving toward your children. Furthermore, your children benefit from learning to accept rules and boundaries; manage their emotions in healthy ways; and gain more confidence in their ability to manage life's ups and downs, all of which are skills with major long-term payoffs.

BOOK STRUCTURE

The first chapter of the book lays out the eight faulty mindsets I have identified that prevent parents from setting loving limits. The remaining chapters address the most common challenges that arise in the early years: cooperation, tantrums, aggression, sleep, potty learning, and feeding. For each of these challenges, I show, through detailed, real-life stories of my work with families, how making important mindshifts can help you respond to the challenges that arise with your children—with all their complexity—in ways that are both loving and effective. You will see how it is possible to be less reactive and thus better able to tune in to the underlying meaning of your child's behavior, what she is struggling with and what she needs from you to better cope. This opens the door to developing strategies that are more sensitive and effective for engaging your child's cooperation, reducing meltdowns and physical aggression, eradicating nighttime and mealtime battles, and helping your child learn to use the potty without power struggles. These stories provide a road map for how you can solve your own child-rearing challenges by adapting the guiding principles and strategies employed throughout this book with your own children in the context of your unique family.

You will see that I have not devoted a specific chapter to discipline. That is because discipline—which is derived from words meaning "to teach"—is part of the fabric of your everyday interactions with your child and is embedded in every story in this book. You are teaching your child to accept life's rules and limits when you stick to a healthy bedtime routine, help him leave the playground to go home for dinner when he still wants more time to play, and don't allow a chocolate energy bar to be a breakfast choice. In this way, discipline is an integral part of each chapter in this book.

While I do not dive deeply into the foundations of young children's development, as a mental health clinician and someone who was steeped in learning and writing about early brain development in my tenure at ZERO TO THREE, the guidance provided in this book is based in science. There are many excellent parenting books out there that do a thorough job of explaining the science of early childhood, which I strongly recommend you check out, especially Tovah Klein's

How Toddlers Thrive, Mona Delahooke's *Beyond Behaviors*, and Dan Siegel and Tina Bryson's *The Whole-Brain Child*. These and other books are listed in the appendix.

In these chapters, you will see how it is possible to establish a warm, nurturing bedtime routine while also setting clear limits in a way that prevents power struggles; how you can have a blast on the playground and then lovingly help your child deal with her disappointment and move on when it's time to leave; and how you can enjoy a fun family meal together without battles over food choices. I hope these stories help you see how changing mindsets empowers you to be the loving, calm, connected, in-charge parents you want to be.

A Note about Highly Sensitive Children

Before diving into this book's core content, it is important to say a few words about children who are highly sensitive (HS) by nature (also known as temperament) because many of them are featured in the scenarios I describe. This is no surprise given that HS children are wired to register their feelings and experiences in the world more deeply than other kids, both emotionally and from a sensory perspective.[1] They tend to experience sights, sounds, tastes, smells, and/or textures more intensely, which means they tend to be more reactive. They get triggered into stress mode more quickly than other children. They get overwhelmed and feel out of control of their big emotions and bodily sensations, which translates into more frequent and intense meltdowns and more difficulty coping with life's inevitable challenges. Sometimes, HS children are referred to as "orchids"[2] because they are affected by and reactive to even minor changes in their environment. They are more vulnerable than the kids we think of as "dandelions," who are easygoing by nature and thrive even in challenging circumstances (which, by the way, makes their parents look soooo good!).

HS kids live in a state of high alert to prepare for and protect themselves from whatever big emotion or event they may be exposed to next. Like Gracie, to cope, they come up with fixed ideas and expectations about how things should be to make daily life more manageable. This makes them inflexible. They have a hard time accepting an alternative way of doing things. You can see how this can lead to a range of challenges around sleep, mealtimes, potty learning, and cooperating with daily routines that, while not exclusive to HS children, occur more frequently and with greater intensity for them.

It is important to keep in mind that temperament is something we are all born with, not something your child chose or that you instilled. It influences the way we process our experiences in the world. It is why some children jump right into new situations and others are anxious and need time to warm up to the unfamiliar. It is why some children go with the flow and weather life's ups and downs with ease, and others have big reactions to seemingly minor events. It is also why siblings can be so different. They grow up in the same family, but their reactions to the very same experiences, such as a move, a loss, or their parents' approach to discipline, may be vastly different based on their temperament.

The high reactivity that is typical of children who have an HS temperament can be very triggering for their parents. If you have an HS child, this makes becoming aware of faulty mindsets especially important so you can avoid going down a path that escalates, rather than reduces, your child's challenging behaviors. (Resources on temperament and specifically on highly sensitive children are listed in the appendix.)

1

THE EIGHT FAULTY MINDSETS

Through my collaboration with hundreds of parents like Aviva and Daniel over the past 30-plus years, I have identified eight mindsets that present obstacles to parents responding to their children in the most loving and effective way during difficult moments. When you become aware of these mindsets—the lens through which you filter and respond to your children's behaviors—you are empowered to make critical mindshifts that help you see your child's behavior more objectively and respond with sensitivity as you help her cope with life's inevitable challenges. Making these key mindshifts proves to be the missing link between knowing and doing.

1. My child is misbehaving on purpose. He should be able to accept limits and exhibit greater self-control.
2. When my child tries to get her way, she is being manipulative.
3. I can control and change my child's feelings and behavior.
4. Experiencing difficult emotions, such as sadness, fear, and anger, is harmful to my child.
5. It is mean and rejecting not to always give my child what he says he wants and needs. The tantrums that ensue when he doesn't get what he wants are detrimental to him.
6. Experiencing failure is harmful for my child.
7. Providing children clear directions and expectations is being harsh and dictatorial.
8. My child harbors malicious intent when she is aggressive with her words and actions.

As we delve into these mindsets, you will see that they are often interconnected. When parents believe that having a tantrum is inherently harmful to their child, it feels especially mean to withhold something their child wants because it often results in a tantrum. If you believe your child is misbehaving on purpose, you are also likely to perceive his strategic behavior—naturally vying for what he wants—as manipulative.

From Mindset to Mindshift

1. My child is misbehaving on purpose. He should be able to accept limits and exhibit greater self-control.

> Kishan takes Seema, his three-year-old daughter, to the pool several times a week in the summer. Even though Kishan gives Seema a five-minute warning before it's time to get out of the pool, when time is up, Seema says she hasn't had enough swimming and needs five more minutes. When Kishan says no, she calls him mean and starts to pout. In a desperate attempt to stave off a tantrum, Kishan relents and gives Seema the extra time, but that changes exactly nothing. Seema still refuses to get out. Kishan tries bribery and threats—she'll get a treat if she gets out, or she'll lose a book at bedtime if she doesn't get out. Nothing works. Eventually, Kishan has to drag Seema out, which is mortifying for him, and, he imagines, pretty embarrassing for Seema too. Kishan starts to dread going to the pool with her and finds every excuse not to go. They spend more time at home doing indoor things. He knows it would be better for his daughter to be outside, using her muscles, learning to swim, and making new friends. He feels frustrated and sad for both of them.

If this scenario sounds familiar, you are not alone. Interactions like this play out every day in families with young children; the child doesn't follow a direction, the parent tries a range of strategies to get the child to cooperate, the child still doesn't comply, the parent loses it and gets punitive, the child melts down, and the parent either feels bad and caves or angrily punishes the child with no positive resolution.

One of the most foundational mindsets at play during these encounters is the parent's belief that her young child should have greater self-control than she is capable of. It's tricky figuring out what is developmentally appropriate. How do you make sense of the fact that your child can repeat the rule aloud but keeps violating it? How can you interpret this behavior as anything but intentional? What brain science tells us is that just because children can verbalize a rule doesn't mean they have the impulse control to follow it.[3] The part of the brain in charge of managing feelings and impulses is still very immature in children under age five. They are not able to stop and think about their feelings; they are functioning from their "downstairs brain," which is driven by impulses and emotions that they act out. Their desire to get what they want when they want it rules the day.[4]

It is also true that young children learn to rely on behaviors that are successful in getting them what they want. If accusing you of being mean or unfair results in more screen time or pool time, as in Seema's case, your child naturally files away these tactics as effective tools for getting what she wants. If making a big ruckus at bedtime results in a quick ticket to getting to sleep in your bed so he doesn't wake up his younger brother, this behavior is reinforced. These kids are not purposefully misbehaving. They are being strategic (more on this below in Mindset #6).

Having appropriate expectations is critical because the meaning you assign to your child's behavior influences how you react. If you think your child is purposefully trying to drive you mad with her defiance, you are much more likely to respond in harsh ways that lead to an increase, not a decrease, in acting-out behavior. When we get revved up and reactive with our young kids, it escalates their distress, making it harder for them to calm down and learn from the experience.[5] If you see these behaviors in the context of normal development, you are more likely to implement limits calmly and with empathy for how hard it is for your child to learn to manage his strong desires and impulses. When you are clear about expectations while remaining loving, you avoid anger and shaming. Your child does not get consumed with upset about the "break" in the relationship with you in that moment and is able to be calm and adapt more quickly.

With this mindshift—*that Seema is driven by her emotions and desires and needs help to learn to follow rules and cope with frustration and disappointment*—Kishan modifies his expectations. He becomes less angry and frustrated and more empathetic about how hard it can be for little Seema, with her three-year-old brain, to manage her emotions. Kishan is now able to accept Seema's disappointment when she has to end a fun activity. He doesn't expect her to be able to pull herself together right away.

The next time this scenario arises with Seema, Kishan responds in a calmer, more effective way. When it's time to come out of the pool, he tells Seema she has two great choices. Either she comes out of the pool on her own or she refuses to come out of the pool, in which case Kishan will be a helper and carry her out. When Seema swims away at Kishan's direction to come out, he calmly steps into the pool to retrieve her. Kishan reminds himself that as unpleasant as tantrums can be, Seema is not misbehaving on purpose and that he doesn't need to be angry at her during these encounters (which he actually finds very freeing). He understands how hard it is for Seema to cope with transitions and limits she doesn't like. Accordingly, he quickly dries her off and ignores her screaming—something he has no control over. He tells her he knows it's hard to leave the pool and then just starts singing one of her favorite songs to show Seema that he is not angry or frustrated. His mindset is that, because he loves her so much, he is not going to engage in a protracted battle. He is just going to help her move on.

Even seeing it through this lens of empathy, carrying Seema out of the pool is no less humiliating. But Kishan reminds himself what the alternative is; this helps him stick to the plan that he knows is right and loving even if her protests feel bad in his gut.

After a few days, the combination of Kishan responding lovingly and calmly and Seema experiencing the natural consequences of her choices yields positive results. Seema more often than not chooses to get out of the pool by herself. Further, the more Kishan uses this approach in other challenging moments with Seema, the less frequent and intense her tantrums become, and the more she begins to cooperate with Kishan's directions, even when she has to transition from a pleasurable activity to a more mundane task.

2. When my child tries to get her way, she is being manipulative.

> Luca and Scott walk into my office and announce that they have a master manipulator living in their home. They explain that they had established what they wanted to be a hard and fast rule that there would be no screen time for their daughter, Sophie (age four), in the mornings before school. But Sophie refuses to get dressed unless they let her watch an episode of Peppa Pig while she puts her clothes on. Every morning, it's the same scenario. Luca and Scott ask Sophie to get dressed. She demands Peppa. They remind her there is no TV in the morning. They tell her they will come back in five minutes and expect her to be dressed. When they return, Sophie is just messing around in her room and announces, "I need Peppa!" They get annoyed and start raising their voices, telling Sophie they are going to be late and that she needs to cooperate! After a prolonged power struggle, the situation always concludes the same way. The clock is ticking, so to get everyone to their destination on time, Luca and Scott give in and turn on the show. They are angry at Sophie for putting them in this position and "extorting" them. They wonder how they have gotten to a point where a four-year-old can wield so much power and control the family in this way.

Interpreting Sophie's behavior as manipulative is a stumbling block for Luca and Scott. It puts them in a negative frame of mind that leads to harsh and threatening tactics, which are backfiring.

The critical mindshift I help them make is *that Sophie is being strategic, not manipulative. She is doing exactly what the DNA of a four-year-old dictates—to find ways to assert control over her world.* Whatever tactics work to achieve her goal—in this case, getting more screen time—are reinforced and go in the "win" column. This ability to assess a situation and figure out how to get what she wants is a skill that will serve Sophie well in life. Luca and

Scott can't stop her from vying for what she wants. What they do have control over is how they respond to Sophie's demands.

With this change in mindset, Luca and Scott are able to make a plan that puts them back in the driver's seat—where they belong—while remaining calm and loving—where they want to be. They let Sophie know that she has "two great choices." She can choose to cooperate with getting dressed, or she can go to school in her pajamas. These are both options that enable them to keep moving along versus waiting for Sophie to agree to cooperate. They are very careful to present these choices matter-of-factly without threats or shaming.

As they had expected, Sophie rejects these choices and has a major meltdown, screaming for Peppa Pig. Luca and Scott remind themselves that they can tolerate the short-term stress of her upset at not getting what she wants in favor of the long-term goal of helping Sophie accept important and appropriate limits. This self-talk enables them to stick to the plan and to remain calm and loving throughout—now that they have a plan that they have the ability to implement. They place her in the car in her pajamas but decide to pack a change of clothes in her backpack in case she changes her mind at school and wants to wear daytime attire. This makes following through on the limit more palatable to them.

After going to school two days in her pajamas (both days she comes home in her daytime clothes; the teacher reports she changes the minute she gets to school), dressing battles cease, and mornings are much more manageable and pleasant for everyone.

3. I can control and change my child's feelings and behavior.

> Finn, age three, is generally a good sleeper. He falls asleep on his own and sleeps through the night. But he wakes up consistently around 5:00 a.m. and comes into his parents' room, ready to roll, even though he hasn't had enough sleep. They try a range of tactics to get him to stay in his room until 6:00 a.m.: logic ("If you stay in bed longer you'll have more energy to play tomorrow"), bribery/rewards ("You can have an extra 30 minutes on the tablet"), and threats ("You'll have no screen

time for a month!"). None of these strategies works. Finn is not swayed by the logic. He is not interested in the reward and is not cowed by the threat. The only way Mitchell and Susannah can eke out a little more shut-eye is by letting Finn climb into bed with them, which they really don't want to do. It makes it impossible for them to go back to sleep. They don't want this to become a habit, but they see it as their only option. They feel totally manipulated by, and angry at, Finn for putting them in this predicament.

One of the key pitfalls Mitchell and Susannah fall into is trying to control Finn's behavior—to *make* him stay in his room until "morning." But the fact is that you cannot actually make your children do anything: eat, sleep, pee on the potty, be kind, or not yell or have a tantrum. Children, like all humans, are the only ones who control their words and actions. This is one of the most humbling aspects of parenting that no one warns you about. It is so fiercely counter to how we see ourselves and our role. We are supposed to be able to *make* our children behave.

But when you focus your efforts on trying to make your child change his behavior, you actually *put him in the driver's seat.* When you are in the position of trying to convince your child to cooperate with a direction or agree to a limit, you are actually ceding control of the situation to him. Think about it—all of the typical tactics we use to try to get children to get with the program put the outcome in their hands. What happens if, like Finn, your child isn't swayed by your logic; he doesn't accept the bribe or reward, or he doesn't fear the threat? Your child remains in control of how the scenario unfolds and gets resolved. In this case, Finn got exactly what he wanted, and Susannah and Mitchell got exactly what they didn't want.

Further, if your child does accept the bribe/reward and agrees to cooperate, he is still establishing the rules of engagement. He will follow a direction or make the right choice only if he receives some reward or special treat for complying. He'll stay in his bed after lights out if he gets more screen time the next morning. He'll sit at the dinner table, but only if he gets three cookies after dinner instead of the two you had determined was acceptable.

The fact is, the more you make it your goal to control your child—to get her to do something—the more *she* is in charge. *Her* behavior determines the outcome of the situation. This is what is so infuriating to parents and leads to reactive, harsh, and ultimately ineffective responses.

This dynamic puts you and your child into what I call the "gray zone," or the no-man's land in which you are trying to get your child to comply with a direction or accept a limit through all of these negotiating and persuasion tactics. Absent clear expectations and boundaries, children are left to their own devices to fill the void and take charge. They make threats ("I won't go to sleep unless you sleep with me"), pull on heartstrings ("But I haven't had enough time with you today, Daddy"), or make you feel you are mistreating them ("You are not being a kind mommy right now"). These kinds of responses then provoke revved-up reactions from parents that further fuel the power struggle.

The other danger of the gray zone is that it descends children deeper into dysregulation. Without the scaffolding that boundaries provide for children, they spiral further out of control. We saw this with Gracie who could get herself into a complete tizzy at book time, demanding "I want daddy . . . no, I want mommy . . . no, I want daddy!" Once Aviva and Daniel set a clear boundary, Gracie was much better able to regulate herself, accept the limit, and move on in a positive way for all.

The critical mindshift Mitchell and Susannah have to make is, *while we can't control Finn, we can control the situation based on how we respond in these moments.* This helps them forgo tactics designed to control Finn in favor of providing him clear choices with natural consequences that Mitchell and Susannah *have the power to implement.*

They get an okay-to-wake clock that has a red light and a green light (see appendix) so Finn has a concrete, visual way of knowing when it is time to stay in bed and when it is okay to get up. They childproof the room to make sure there is nothing that could cause danger if Finn is in there by himself for any period of time. They help Finn create a morning box with quiet toys to play with until the clock is green. They explain that, if he gets up and the light is still red, it is his job to either go back to sleep or play quietly until the light is green. (Mitchell and Susannah are now keenly aware that they cannot make Finn go back to sleep, so they don't focus on or dictate that.) They explain that, if he chooses to come out of the room before the green light is on, they will escort him back to his room. The rule is everyone stays in their own bed until 6:00 a.m. and they are going to be sticking to that.

The first morning Mitchell and Susannah implement the plan, Finn comes into their room at 5:00 a.m. Calmly and without saying a word, Susannah escorts him back to his room. She offers to tuck him back in, but Finn starts to run around the room to evade Susannah. Susannah does not react. She blows Finn a kiss and says she can't wait to see him when the clock turns green. Finn continues to come out of the room. Susannah silently and calmly walks him back. (This is no small feat because Finn tries to prompt interaction—asking Susannah questions and being silly and charming—to get his mom engaged.) When the clock finally turns green, Finn comes out, gets Susannah, and they go into the family room to play quietly together.

The next two mornings are repeats. On the fourth morning, Finn starts calling out to Susannah and Mitchell at around 5:30, but he doesn't come into their room until the clock turns green. When he arrives at their bed, he proudly announces "I did it! I waited for the green light!" And that was the end of the morning madness. Some mornings, they find Finn playing and talking to his animals before the clock turns green. (An added benefit of this new plan is that Finn has learned how to entertain himself.) But, more and more frequently, he sleeps until or past 6:00 a.m.

Experiencing the positive power of this plan for addressing the sleep problem, Mitchell and Susannah start to take a similar approach to other power struggles they have with Finn. They didn't have these challenges with their older son, Sean, who is much more laid back, and so they had not developed the tools they needed to effectively support a more fierce, persistent child. They had been feeling terrible and were concerned about Finn being pigeonholed as the "difficult" kid. They are thrilled to have forged a more positive and loving connection with him.

Becoming aware of and accepting that you can't control your children but you can control the situation enables you to focus on changing your reactions in a way that reduces power struggles and engages your children's cooperation.

4. Experiencing difficult emotions, such as sadness, fear, and anger, is harmful to my child.

> Alana, age six, and her mom, Stephanie, are moving to a new home. This means Alana will be starting kindergarten in a new school. Alana tells her mom that she doesn't want to leave her current school and friends. Stephanie reassures Alana that she will love the new school—that they have a much bigger playground and a music class (Alana's favorite) two times a week, whereas her current school has music only once a week. The more Stephanie tries to reassure Alana, the more Alana ups the ante. She proclaims that the new school is stupid, that none of the kids will like her, and that she no longer likes music. (The lengths kids will go to get their point across!) Stephanie is getting increasingly worried that Alana is setting herself up for failure and feels helpless as to how to help her make a healthy adaptation to the new school.

Stephanie's reaction is rooted in the faulty mindset that experiencing difficult emotions is inherently harmful to children. As a loving parent, her impulse is to make the bad feelings go away. She unconsciously filters Alana's fear, sadness, and anger through the faulty mindset that having a happy child means she needs to be happy all the time. (Something I still struggle with despite having very grown children who live outside my home!) To reduce our children's (and our own) distress, we try to make the feelings smaller or go away altogether by minimizing, ignoring, or trying to talk our children out of their difficult feelings: "Don't be sad;

Grandma will visit another day," or "You'll love the new school; there are so many more toys there." These tactics don't make the feelings go away; they just send a message to the child that we are uncomfortable with her difficult emotions, which prevents her from having a healthy outlet to work through her feelings. Instead, the feelings get acted out through behaviors that can lead to more, not less, stress for children and parents.

The mindshift to make is that *feelings in and of themselves are not harmful to children.* Sadness and joy, anger and love can coexist and are part of the collection of emotions that make us human and add color and richness to our lives. It is learning to accept and manage their full range of emotions that makes children happy, because they are ready for anything. They are equipped to successfully navigate life's ups and downs and feel confident to master the challenges they face as they grow. Our job is not to rid or protect our children from their difficult emotions; it is to show we trust that they can learn to manage them with our help. And it starts with nonjudgmental acknowledgment and acceptance of their feelings and experiences.

With this mindshift, Stephanie changes her approach. When Alana expresses difficult feelings, Stephanie acknowledges and validates them. She tells Alana that she understands that leaving her old school and friends is really hard and that feeling sad and angry about the change makes a lot of sense to her. She encourages Alana to talk about the things she will miss. When Alana makes negative (and often totally irrational) proclamations about the new school, Stephanie does not react to them at face value nor try to correct or discount them. Instead of responding "But you love music!," Stephanie responds with "Tell me more about that. I want to understand." Stephanie also shares some of her own experiences of change and loss and how she coped with these transitions to show Alana that she is not alone.

Only after Stephanie has encouraged Alana to express her feelings fully does Stephanie move to problem solving. She asks Alana for her ideas about how she can stay connected to her friends. Together, they brainstorm a list of things Alana can do to keep her old friends and school in her heart and mind, for example, making a photo album and establishing ways to keep in touch through video chats and sending photos and letters to each other via their parents' email. This new approach helps Alana have a more positive mindset about the new school and sets her up for a successful transition.

5. It is mean and rejecting to not always give my child what he says he wants and needs. The tantrums that ensue when he doesn't get what he wants are harmful to him.

> Cherie is in charge of the bedtime routine with three-year-old Kai. She treasures this experience because, with her demanding job, it is the only time of day when Cherie has a good stretch of time with Kai. Cherie's favorite part of the routine is after lights out when they have cuddle time for 10 minutes before she says her final good night.
>
> Recently, when the 10 minutes are up, Kai has started insisting he has "just one more question!" Cherie relents. One question quickly turns into three, four, five, or more questions. Cherie, on the one hand, knows this is not a good dynamic— that Kai is trying to delay bedtime and it's working. On the other hand—the heavier hand—it feels mean and rejecting to refuse to answer Kai's questions. She asks herself what kind of message this would be sending him. She keeps waiting for Kai to say it's enough—that he's satisfied—so they can separate for the night in a loving way and avoid the tantrum that will likely ensue if she sticks to the 10-minute limit.
>
> But then comes the inevitable point when Cherie cracks. Kai's persistence in pushing the limit is making Cherie angry at him for putting her in a situation where she feels mean about cutting him off. She snaps and shouts, "It's never enough for you!" Kai pleads, "Don't be angry, Mommy." Cherie slumps in despair. All she wants is a loving, peaceful time with her little one, so she caves. Bedtime extends 30 minutes past the time Kai should be going to sleep and ends with his falling asleep with her by his side, despite her goal of having him be able to fall asleep on his own. Cherie is desperate to turn this around, but night after night it's the same story. She feels powerless and paralyzed.

If you're like many of the parents I consult with every day, you are quickly triggered to feel you are being mean when your child is upset that you won't read that sixth book at bedtime ("just one more and then I'll go to sleep!"), prepare a third meal after she has rejected the first two options (that *she* had requested), or let him have just five more minutes to finish his game (which ultimately turns into an additional 20 minutes of screen time). This mindset makes it very challenging to follow through with setting and enforcing the limits children desperately need but don't necessarily love.

The problem is that a lack of limits puts your child in charge. When kids are calling the shots, it makes you feel out of control, manipulated, and angry, which results in exactly the scenario you are so desperately trying to avoid—acting "mean." You lose it and start yelling, shaming, and punishing, which leaves everyone feeling miserable and your child having learned little about developing better coping skills.

The necessary mindshift is that, *just because your child doesn't love a limit, doesn't mean it's not good for him and that the tantrums that ensue when a child doesn't get something he wants doesn't mean they are detrimental to him.* Helping your child learn to cope with not getting everything he wants is loving, not harmful. It leads to flexibility and the development of effective coping strategies. Observe any childcare center or preschool class and you will see how children learn to accept limits: not being the line leader or snack helper, having to lie down on a cot for an hour for rest time, or needing to share their favorite toy. This ability to adapt is what ultimately makes children happy and helps them be successful in the outside world, now and in the future.

Once you see that your child's distress at not getting what she wants is temporary and that it is actually helping her build strong coping skills, you will feel much more comfortable asserting your authority appropriately. Remember, kids have parents for a reason. Otherwise, it would be *Lord of the Flies*. Kids would eat tons of junk food, be on screens all day, and stay up until the wee hours. It is your job to set the limits that keep them safe and teach them to ultimately make good decisions as they grow.

This means not falling into the trap of trying to convince your child to agree to your limits. In over three decades of working with kids and families, I have yet to hear a child say thank you for limiting screen time so he can engage in more fortifying activities or agree to three instead of four books at bedtime because it's really important for him to get to bed on time. So, when your child protests your excellent parenting decision, let her know that you hear she doesn't like or agree with your rule and that you don't expect her to. Why would she be happy about book time ending or having to leave the playground when she is having so much fun? Be clear that it is your job to set limits that keep her healthy and safe so you will still be enforcing them and it's okay if she is mad or frustrated about it. You have full confidence that she will learn to manage when she can't have something she wants.

With this mindshift, Cherie is able to make a very effective course correction. She uses a clearly visible timer to show Kai exactly how much cuddle time is remaining. When the timer beeps, she gives him a special good-night kiss and leaves the room. She also tells Kai that he has a special place in his brain—his "memory brain"—where he can store all the questions he has that they don't have time to get to and that she can't wait to hear all about at breakfast. This gives Kai a concrete tool for coping with the limit she is setting and provides a positive focus as they separate.

Naturally, Kai tests the first night, chasing after Cherie multiple times to get her to come back after lights out. Cherie has to physically pick him up and take him back to his room. She also decides to put up a boundary to help him stay in his room. This feels really uncomfortable to her. It is hard to hold onto the idea that implementing these limits is loving to Kai when his reaction seems to convey the exact opposite. She has to keep asking herself, "What's the alternative?" As hard as this is, going back to the old dynamic is not a loving response. This helps her stick to the plan. On night three, Kai's protests end as he adapts to the new system. Cherie feels tremendous relief that the final hour of each day with Kai is calm and loving, not full of anger and stress.

6. Experiencing failure is harmful for my child.

> Five-year-old Jamal has a low tolerance for frustration. The second he faces a challenge—like not being able to find exactly where the puzzle piece fits—he melts down and gives up. His dad, Khalil, worries that the distress Jamal experiences when he can't master a task right away is harmful and erodes his self-confidence. Khalil jumps in to solve the problem to relieve Jamal's stress.

This impulse—to rescue our children when they struggle—is a natural, human reaction. Our knee-jerk response is to fix whatever is causing our children distress. The mindshift to make is *that learning a new skill involves feeling uncomfortable to some degree until we have mastered it. Struggling is not bad or harmful for children. It is part of the learning process.* The stress children experience as they work through a challenge is what we call positive stress because it leads to growth.[6] Picture your child working on riding a bicycle. If you never let up on your hold—always doing the balancing for her—she won't experience the teetering that can feel a little scary and uncomfortable. But that is what leads her to figure out how to eventually maintain her balance and feel the incredible sense of pride when she can cruise around on her own.

After, when we run to the rescue, we are sending the message that we don't think our kids are capable of mastering the challenges they face and that only adults can solve their problems. It teaches them that failure is something to be feared or ashamed of when in fact it is a critical component of growth and development. While it is no doubt easier to swoop in as the fixer, acting as a supportive coach is what builds your child's self-confidence and helps her learn to muscle through life's challenges.

After making this mindshift—getting comfortable with Jamal's discomfort—Khalil takes a new approach. He now acknowledges Jamal's frustration without judgment or criticism, and he doesn't try to make it all better. He offers Jamal help to persevere in trying to solve the problem, for example, by guiding him to try different spaces in the puzzle or turning the pieces around to see them from a different perspective. When Jamal goes from zero to 60, Khalil refrains from trying to cajole or cheerlead Jamal to persevere. He knows that, in these moments, Jamal's brain is closed and can't process any information or ideas. Any prodding by Khalil only escalates Jamal's distress. Instead, Khalil helps Jamal take a break. Together, they come up with a great tool to help Jamal when he is starting to get agitated. Jamal announces, "Houston, we have a problem" to signal that he needs help, instead of just melting down. This new approach results in a significant shift in Jamal's reaction when he confronts a challenge. He falls apart much less frequently and has begun to show clear signs of increasing confidence in himself as a competent problem solver.

7. Telling my child what to do is being dictatorial.

> On a home visit recently, Julia asks her four-year-old, Marley, "Please don't throw the ball against the wall, okay?" After several requests without a response, Marley turns to Julia and simply states, "No, I like throwing it at the wall." I ask Julia whether she intended this to be a question or a direction. Julia explains that it is a rule she wants to enforce but she doesn't like telling her kids what to do. It makes her feel like a harsh dictator. She prefers to give her children choices.

This is a sentiment I have heard from many parents. Giving explicit directions feels uncomfortable, which results in their unconsciously, but persistently, posing what they intend as directions as questions: "Can you put your toys away?" or "Time to get pj's on, okay?" This is confusing to children; they hear that they are being given a choice even though this is not their parents' intention. When children don't comply, parents get frustrated and angry. Children in turn are bewildered by their parents' punitive reactions.

No doubt, giving children choices is very important, but not everything is a choice, for example, getting in the car seat. That is a direction, not a choice. It might go something like this: "It's time to get into the car seat. That is going to happen because it is my job to keep you safe. How it happens is up to you. You can climb in on your own, or I will be a helper and place you in. You decide." Children thrive on having clear directions. That is why they are often more cooperative at school where their marching orders are crystal clear, which makes them feel safe and secure. Teachers don't ask children if they'd like to clean up or to make space in the circle for another friend. Children understand that these are directions to follow, not to discuss, debate, or opt out of. There is no gray zone.

The mindshift to make is that *knowing exactly what is expected provides children the information they need to feel secure in the world and to be successful.* When the expectations and directions aren't clear and you are in the gray zone, it's hard for children to make good choices. Kids have parents for a reason; they need you to be in charge. Don't fear your power. It is possible to be a strong, trusted authority figure while maintaining a loving connection with your child. The stories throughout this book will show you how.

Once Julia becomes conscious that functioning from this mindset is making things harder, not easier, for Marley, she is able to be more effective in engaging Marley's cooperation. She explains to her the difference between a choice and a direction. A choice is something Marley gets to pick; a direction is a must—something she has to do. Balls don't get thrown at the wall—that is a direction. The choice is to roll them along the floor or toss them into a basket. If Marley has a hard time following the rule, the ball goes away for a period of time. She will always get another chance to try again and make a different choice.

8. My child harbors malicious intent when she is aggressive with her words and actions.

> Harrison has a ritual with Lucas, his five-year-old. Every night when Harrison arrives home from work, they play in the back-yard. They both love this special time together. But, inevitably, when it's time to go inside for dinner, Lucas puts up a fight. Harrison is good about giving Lucas a two-minute warning, but that doesn't head off the tantrum. Neither does Harrison's agreeing to Lucas's pleas for a little extra time. But it's never enough. When Harrison finally starts to walk back into the house to show Lucas that playtime is really done, Lucas shouts: "You are a mean daddy poopy face." Harrison, fuming, turns around and retorts: "How dare you speak to me that way! There won't be any more playtime when I come home from work if you keep that up!" Lucas storms past Harrison, runs into the house, and exclaims that he's never talking to his dad again.
>
> Harrison and his wife, Jill, are at a loss as to how to handle these outbursts, which are happening with increasing fre-quency. Every time Lucas doesn't get his way, he starts to hurl vitriol. They wonder how two caring, kind people like themselves are raising such a rude, disrespectful child. They don't know how to stop him from spewing this venom. No punishment (sending him to his room) or threat (to take things away) is making a difference.

Children making alarming threats and aggressive statements is not a new phenomenon. Kids have been known to say a lot of outra-geous things when they are angry or frustrated. While provocative statements and threats, especially coming from such a young child, feel so wrong, it's important not to interpret and react to these inflammatory and provocative exclamations at face value. Chil-dren don't always literally mean what they say. Your child is not a budding sociopath. The stress at not getting something he wants has activated his downstairs brain, and he is purging emotion.

While your logical reaction might be that you need to teach your child a lesson through some kind of disciplinary action that shames or punishes him for this inappropriate outburst, when you react harshly, it can escalate, rather than reduce, the distress your child is experiencing that led to the inappropriate proclamation to begin with. A big reaction also teaches your child that this kind of vitriol gets a reaction. So, when your child is mad at you for depriving him of something he desires, these provocative statements now become effective strategies to get your attention and yank your chain, which results in more of these surly (or "obnoxious," as one parent recently put it) statements.

The same is true for physical aggression in young children. Much of the time, hitting, biting, and kicking are reflexive reactions that your child can't control. Even when it seems more purposeful, for example, when your child hits you because you won't give him more TV time, he doesn't really want to *hurt* you. The downstairs brain has kicked into high gear, which results in a physiological response.

This is not to say that aggressive behavior is acceptable. It's not, and we need to help kids learn to manage their feelings in appropriate ways. But, if you react to these incidents from a mindset that your child is being purposefully malicious, your response is more likely to be harsh and punitive, which only tends to beget more aggressive behavior. The chapter on aggressive behavior goes deep on how important mindshifts can help you respond to physical outbursts in a loving and effective way.

With this important change in mindset—*that Lucas is not intentionally being hurtful*—Harrison and Jill adopt a new tactic when Lucas uses inappropriate language. They ignore the unacceptable statements but don't ignore Lucas. They acknowledge the underlying feeling or issue Lucas is struggling with and then focus on engaging him in something positive and productive.

In the situation described above, the redo goes something like this: When Lucas starts to get agitated and say unacceptable things, Harrison stays calm and connected. He empathizes with Lucas's disappointment when they have to stop playing to start dinner. They have so much fun together; it's a very special time they both look forward to. Then, Harrison heads into the house. When Lucas starts up with the verbal attacks, Harrison calmly lets Lucas know that, when he is ready, daddy can't wait to have a helper in the kitchen. Harrison doesn't say anything about the vitriol, and he doesn't try to talk Lucas out of being upset. Harrison knows that an important part of his job is to allow Lucas the space to learn to cope with these kinds of inevitable disappointments, such as when a fun activity has to end. Further, getting overinvolved in trying to make it all better sends Lucas the message that Harrison doesn't think Lucas can manage these difficult moments. (You see how the mindshifts are often interrelated. In our work together, Harrison and Jill had come to recognize that allowing Lucas to have his difficult feelings isn't harmful, but is instead helpful, and that they are not being mean nor rejecting by setting appropriate limits.) By responding in this way, Harrison is, in effect, saying to Lucas, "I love you so much that I will not fuel this flame by reacting angrily or by participating in an unhealthy power struggle." While Lucas continues to try to provoke his dad, Harrison does not react. He starts helping Jill work on dinner and periodically mentions how much he'd love a helper to place the broccoli on the baking sheet. Eventually, Lucas saunters over and gets to work in the kitchen—an activity he loves.

This kind of response is the most powerful and positive way to communicate to children that they are seen and understood—what they want and need most—while also teaching them the rules of engagement—what behaviors are acceptable and not acceptable. The goal is to be responsive; to show empathy for your child's struggle while maintaining the limit, not to be reactive, which just escalates the negative encounter and reinforces the unwanted behavior.

The chapters that follow take a deep dive into how these mindsets are at play in challenging moments with children and how making important mindshifts—seeing the situation through a "corrective lens"—can help you do the seemingly impossible: manage your emotions so you can respond in ways that are calm, loving, sensitive, *and* effective.

We begin with cooperation because, when it comes down to it, that's the ultimate goal parents are aiming for—whether it be to get a child to sit at the dinner table, to stay in her room after lights out, use the potty for her pee and poop, or get dressed in the morning without a knock-down-drag-out fight.

2

COOPERATION

Doug and Prudence are fed up. Mornings with Maggie, their four-year-old, have become a nightmare. From the moment she wakes up until they leave the house for school and work, they are pulling teeth to get her through the four tasks that have to be accomplished: getting dressed, eating breakfast, brushing teeth, and getting into the car seat. Maggie protests every step. It starts with her yelling for them to come get her when she wakes up, only to be met with "go away!" the second they appear. When they walk out in the face of her rejection, Maggie screams for them to return. The more they try to coax and cajole her into a better mood, the more out of sorts she gets. They have started to give her the tablet to watch a show because that is the only thing that gets her to calm down and move on with the morning tasks.

When the show is over, they tell her that it is time to get dressed and that they will be back in 10 minutes and expect the clothes she picked out the night before to be on. When they return to check on her, Maggie hasn't made any progress. They bribe her again by telling her she can have another show if she gets her clothes on and brushes her teeth. The grand finale is carrying her to the car, kicking and screaming. It is a miserable situation for everyone.

One of the most common complaints from parents who come to see me for consultation is "My child won't listen." Typical grievances include "Ethan whines and protests every single step of the bedtime routine." "Talia's refusal to cooperate is forcing us to nag and bribe her, which is driving us crazy and we know is messed up. We're all hating on each other by the time we walk out the door in the morning." "Caitlyn just does what she wants to do. She wants to be the boss of everything, and it turns out that she is, in fact, the boss of everything."

MINDSETS THAT GET IN THE WAY OF ENGAGING YOUR CHILD'S COOPERATION

I find that there are a series of faulty mindsets at play that interfere with parents' ability to effectively engage their children's cooperation.

My Child Is Misbehaving on Purpose

It feels like your child is intentionally trying to drive you mad. I often hear exasperated parents wondering "Why can't she just put on her clothes, which would take all of two minutes, rather than drawing us into a protracted power struggle that makes everyone miserable?" The problem is that you are looking at these scenarios from a logical perspective. Your child is not.

For one, children are driven to assert some control over their world. This means that whenever a demand is made to follow someone else's agenda, there is a natural tendency to defy it. This is especially true for kids who are more inflexible than easygoing by nature—they have a particularly fierce need for control.

It is also hard for many children to move from one activity to another. They become absorbed in what they are doing. Making a transition takes a lot of effort, and some children are more distractible than others. They start to follow a direction, but something catches their attention and they lose track of what they are supposed to be focused on.

In other cases, the root cause for the lack of cooperation might be that your child has not tuned in to what you are communicating to her. Without realizing it, many of us talk to children before securing their full attention. How often do you find yourself repeating a direction, calling your child's name over and over, rephrasing the same direction 10 different ways, or talking to the back of your child's head while he's focused on something else? If your child hasn't processed the information you are communicating, it makes it difficult for her to act effectively on your direction. There are certainly times when children are purposefully ignoring your direction because they have learned that this is a good strategy to avoid having to make a transition (not because they are trying to work your last nerve). There are also times when children are not focusing on you because they get so absorbed in their own internal experience that they have a hard time turning their attention to what others are trying to communicate to them. Ensuring that your child has actually heard your direction is a critical step.

Finally, when it comes to morning and nighttime routines, children may be especially resistant to complying with the necessary tasks because they are associated with separations. The morning routine ultimately concludes with having to say goodbye to Mom and Dad as they go off to childcare or school. The bedtime routine ends with having to separate for the night. These transitions can be emotionally challenging for young children.

Being aware of the possible underlying feelings and motivations at play for your child when she is faced with a direction or limit can help you respond in a way that is both empathetic and effective in helping her cooperate, as you will see from the stories below.

Telling My Child What to Do Is Being Dictatorial

As I began to do more and more home visits, I noticed the frequent phenomenon of parents feeling uncomfortable giving their children clear and specific directions. When they wanted their child to get into his pajamas, instead of saying "It's time to get into your pj's," they'd say either "Can you get into you pj's?" or "It's time to get into your pj's, *okay?*" Instead of "Time to get into your car seat," they'd say "Are you ready to get in the car seat?" On one home visit, a mom kept asking her two-year-old to "Please take your feet off the kitchen table, *okay?*" After several requests, the toddler turned to her mom and simply said, "No, I like them on the table." Here's another recent example: A mom asked her four-year-old multiple times, "Can you please come to the dinner table?" The child (logically) responded, "No, I'm not done with my game." Parents were posing what they intended to be directions as conciliatory questions totally unconsciously. But the net effect was that it was leading to constant power struggles when their children, who were getting the message that they had some say in the matter, responded with a resounding no either verbally or by not following through with the request.

This mindset proves to be a core obstacle to parents being effective in getting their kids to cooperate. When I ask parents what makes it uncomfortable to give a direction, it becomes clear that telling their kids what to do flies in the face of their belief that children should be given choices and not be dictated to. It also makes them feel like they are being harsh with their child. In fact, giving children clear directions is helpful, not harmful. Clarity is king. It is confusing to children when the expectations aren't clear. Children do need choices, lots of them, but within appropriate limits. It is not a choice to clean up toys—that is a direction. The choice might be to put away the blocks first or the cars. Getting in the car seat is a direction. The choice is whether your child climbs in on his own or you are a helper and secure him in. These are appropriate choices within a larger, overarching limit that you set as a parent. *Don't confuse giving clear directions with depriving your child of a sense of agency.*

To take this even one step further, when setting a limit, it can be very helpful to give voice to the fact that you *don't* expect your child to like or agree with your limit. "We aren't going to get any sweets today at the store. I know how much you love treats, and the last time we went to the store I let you get some candy. But today we are getting just healthy foods. It's totally fine if you don't like this decision. I don't expect you to. But it's a mommy/daddy job to make the rules about food." Putting it on the table matter-of-factly communicates to your child that you don't fear his protest or tantrum and you accept and understand that he is upset (something that, remember, you have no control over). This can go a long way toward preempting and diffusing your child's protests. It is also an honest and respectful way to validate his experience and let him know that you are not afraid of his feelings and that you have faith that he can eventually accept and cope with whatever frustration or disappointment he has experienced.

I Can Control and Change My Child's Behavior

If you are like most parents, you probably find yourself doing a fair amount of nagging despite your distaste for it. You may be using rewards and/or bribery (which are really the same thing) and threats of taking away desired toys or activities to incentivize your child to change her behavior. But, remember, all of these strategies put you in the position of waiting for your child to agree to comply: to accept the bribe or be cowed by the threat. Depending on your child to follow through puts him, not you, in the driver's seat. This means he is the decider about whether or not a task is done. *Your child is not being manipulative; he is being strategic*—another important mindshift to make. Children are driven to pursue their agendas, which might mean trying to prolong breakfast to avoid the inevitable separation when it's time to go to school or refusing to hand over the tablet because what child wants to end screen time? It is our job as the grown-ups to set the appropriate limits to ensure children's overall health and well-being.

Also, keep in mind that when you approach these moments in a revved-up state, making threats like, "If you don't stay in your room, I am going to put up a gate!" or "If you don't put all these toys away, I am throwing them in the trash," it backfires because children pick up on the negativity and react to it. It sends them the message that you are already anticipating that they aren't going to comply and that you are in for a fight. This puts kids in a defiant, power-struggle mode, especially children who are more oppositional by nature. Negativity and threats tend to amplify their resistance. They just dig in their heels more firmly, not to mention that most of the time they know you have no intention of following through on the threat.

The antidote is to turn threats into choices and be sure the choices you offer lead to the outcome you are seeking. Say your child is fighting getting into the bath. You can't *force* her to climb in, but what you can do is explain that "It is time to get washed up. You have two great choices. You can cooperate with getting into the tub safely and have your bath, or I will be a helper and give you a sponge bath. You decide." If she chooses to cooperate, awesome. If she continues to protest and obfuscate, you have a plan that still enables you to get her clean that doesn't depend on her compliance. One habit that can be helpful to get into is to always start by asking yourself *what you do and don't control in the situation at hand*. This can prevent you from falling into the abyss of focusing on trying to change your child, and instead focus on changing your approach.

As you read the stories that follow, you will see how these key factors figure into the cooperation conundrum many parents face.

MAGGIE: MORNING MADNESS

Let's think back to Maggie and the morning madness.

The Mindsets and Mindshifts

As we do the detective work to figure out what is driving the current dynamic, we start by homing in on expectations. Doug and Prudence believe that by age four, Maggie should be able to follow simple directions and go through the morning routine that is the same every day. *Interpreting her behavior as purposefully defiant and manipulative is leading them down a path that is only perpetuating power struggles.* Once they become open to seeing that *Maggie is not "misbehaving" on purpose,* they no longer feel so annoyed and are able to think more clearly about what the root cause of the morning madness might be.

This mindshift leads to an important insight that mornings are hard for Maggie because she has difficulty making "state changes"—going from awake to asleep and asleep to awake. These physiological transitions are uncomfortable for her. When she wakes up out of sorts, it is especially hard for her to get through daily tasks. Doug and Prudence begin to see that this is a feature of Maggie's overall sensitive temperament. She experiences everything intensely, both emotionally and physically, which makes transitions hard for her. They also notice that the more they try to get Maggie to snap out of her bad mood, the more distressed she gets. As counterintuitive as it feels, they see that the more they try to make it all better, the more dysregulated she gets. This insight enables Doug and Prudence *to shift their focus from trying to control Maggie's behavior to how they can respond in a way that actually helps her feel calm and back in control of her mind and body, that they have the power to implement.* They recast their role from being "enforcers" to being helpers. This sets them up to respond more calmly, lovingly, and effectively.

Taking a careful look at how their morning interactions with Maggie unfold, Doug and Prudence also begin to see that *using bribery and threats is landing them squarely in the "gray zone"—the no-man's land where the expectations aren't clear and Maggie is engaged in all sorts of strategies to try to control the situation.* Not only does this propel her deeper into dysregulation, this dynamic amplifies, rather than reduces, the power struggles. Doug and Prudence see that they need to set clearer boundaries to provide the "scaffolding" Maggie needs to get back to a calm place and be able to move forward in a positive way, in other words, to self-regulate.

The Plan

They show empathy and validation. They tell Maggie that they know waking up is hard—that it takes her body and mind time to feel comfortable after a long night of sleep. To help her with this, they have a new, fun plan. They are going to let her choose an additional book at bedtime. They will read it halfway through before lights-out. In the morning, when Maggie wakes up, Mom or Dad will enter her room quietly and finish the book. This will help her wake up more gradually. If on some mornings even this turns out to be too stimulating, they will just sit quietly in her room and wait until she is calm. If she is raging at them, they will wait on the other side of the door. They will know she is ready to have them come back in when they hear her count to 20 (she is really into numbers). This strategy is designed to give Maggie some sense of control over when she is ready to engage.

They make a rule of no screen time in the mornings. Doug and Prudence decide that the option of getting to watch shows in the morning is ultimately not reducing stress but increasing it. They let Maggie know exactly when she *will* be able to watch a show—while Mom and Dad are making dinner.

They provide tools to help Maggie cope. They make a visual schedule to provide a concrete tool to guide Maggie through the morning routine. They take multiple photos of each task: dad and mom reading to her next to her bed at wake-up time, getting dressed, eating breakfast, brushing teeth, and getting into the car. As part of the bedtime routine, they have Maggie pick out two outfits for the next day. In the morning, she can make her final decision about which one to wear.

They also take photos of the two breakfast choices she will have the next morning. The idea is to queue up the choices the night before instead of in the morning when she has a much more difficult time making decisions in the heat of the moment. Every morning, the parent who reads the wake-up book with Maggie takes out all the photos and helps Maggie put the schedule together. They tape the photos that represent each task onto poster board in the order that they happen. (Some families get fancy and use Velcro.) It is at that point that Maggie chooses the photo of the outfit she will wear and the breakfast choice she wants and tapes them onto the schedule.

They provide clear directions. Doug and Prudence assign time limits for each task, for example, 10 minutes to get dressed, 20 minutes for breakfast, and 5 minutes to brush teeth. They use a timer that visibly shows time elapsing. (The time is depicted in color and gradually gets smaller as time passes. You'll find several options when you do an online search. I find the visual timers are much more effective than those that have just numbers or even sand timers, which are harder for young children to track.) They explain to Maggie that, if she completes the task in the time allotted, there will be extra time before leaving for school to play a math game on the computer with her dad, one of her favorite activities. (Cooperation translates into more time for pleasurable activities.) If she doesn't complete a task in the time allotted, there won't be time for the math game.

They provide reasonable choices without ceding control to Maggie. When it comes to getting dressed, they decide that Maggie's two great choices will be to either put on the outfit that she included on the schedule or wear her pajamas to school. They are very careful to present these options very matter-of-factly, not in a shaming tone. Doug and Prudence are clear that they will not get into a battle with her about dressing. They emphasize that it is in her control. It is her decision. To further ensure that this tactic serves as a natural consequence and not a shaming punishment, they pack the outfit she put on the schedule in her backpack so that she can change at school if she wants to.

They establish and adhere to appropriate limits. At breakfast time, they stick to the food choice she made when she put together her schedule. They use a visual timer so Maggie can see exactly how much time she has for breakfast. If she chooses not to eat during that time, they put the food in her backpack in case she changes her mind and wants to eat on the way to school.

They are clear about directions versus choices. When it comes to brushing teeth, they explain to her that this is not a choice, but a direction. They know she doesn't like it, and they totally understand that. They are not asking her to like it. (They have already let her choose from a range of toothbrushes and toothpastes, so they have covered all the bases on that front.) Teeth have to be brushed. How they get brushed is totally up to her. She can do it on her own, or mommy/daddy will do it.

They take the same approach for getting into the car seat. That is a direction, not a choice. She has to be buckled in safely. How she gets in is her choice. She can do it on her own or they will be her helpers and place her in the seat.

They present all of this in the most positive, upbeat tone. They avoid making any threats; they provide clear directions and clear choices.

The Outcome

The night before they enact the new plan, Doug and Prudence remind Maggie that there won't be any screens in the morning and ask her to choose the book she'd like to start now and finish in the morning. She cries that it isn't fair—she needs to have her show in order to wake up! Doug and Prudence stay calm and acknowledge her disappointment but are clear that they are going to stick to the new plan. They let her know they will wait until she chooses the special book to read. They sit quietly and don't react to Maggie's protests about the new screen limit. Mom and Dad talk to each other about the books they see on the shelf and wonder aloud which one Maggie might choose. They use a lot of humor. They pull out one of her favorite books from the shelf and pronounce: "I don't think Maggie will choose this one—she hates this book!" After about five minutes of this kind of banter between mom and dad and their *not* focusing on trying to get Maggie to get with the program, she takes a book off the shelf and hands it to Doug to read—one power struggle averted.

The first morning is very tough. Prudence arrives at Maggie's room with the book in hand. Maggie immediately starts shouting for the tablet. Doug and Prudence are expecting this reaction; they know that the changes they are making are going to be uncomfortable for Maggie and it will take time for her to adapt. But they are committed to the plan. They keep asking themselves what the alternative is as a reminder that the old regime was not helpful to Maggie—it only caused her to spiral further out of control.

Prudence sits quietly and starts to read the book, showing Maggie with her actions that she is sticking to the no-screen rule and that she is going to finish the book they started the night before as planned. She is not going to fan the flames by getting into a discussion about the screen.

When Prudence finishes the book, she takes out the visual schedule. Maggie says she is not going to make any choices, so the first morning she ends up going to school in her pj's and with a baggie of granola that Doug and Prudence choose for her since she refuses to make a decision about what to eat, too. They go through these steps with all the calm they can muster. They acknowledge Maggie is having a hard time—that mornings can be tough. Their job to help her go through each step in the process to get to school on time and they have confidence she can muscle through.

Following this plan consistently, by the third morning they begin to see change. Maggie accepts the "wake-up book" most mornings. There are still days when she is cranky and tells Mom and Dad to go away; but these instances are fewer and further between. Doug also comes up with a great new option. Maggie can choose to finish the book from the night before *or* hear about one of his escapades from childhood—which she can't get enough of. In the mornings when she is angsty, hearing one of his tales snaps her out of it pretty quickly.

Maggie also starts to engage with the visual schedule, with uneven results. Some mornings, she sticks to the choice she makes about what to wear. Other days, she refuses and wants to go into her closet and start the whole selection process over again. Doug and Prudence stick to the plan, which means that, some mornings, Maggie leaves the house kicking and screaming that she doesn't want to wear pajamas to school. Fortunately, they find out from Maggie's teacher that, most days, when she shows up in pajamas, she changes on her own within minutes of her arrival. Other times, she is fine in her pj's. Either way, what's most important is that power struggles over dressing in the morning are averted. By the end of the first month, about 90 percent of the time Maggie cooperates with the plan and wears the outfit she had chosen.

The same is true for breakfast. Some mornings, Maggie accepts the option she put on her schedule; other days, she rejects it and demands a different breakfast. On those mornings, Maggie will say she will never eat what they have packed for her to take to school. Being responsive, not reactive, Doug and Prudence respond with "Okay, sweetie, it is your body and your choice." With no opportunity to delay departure by throwing a tantrum over breakfast, Maggie often ends up eating on the way to school.

Toothbrushing is tough. It is extremely uncomfortable for Doug and Prudence to feel like they are manhandling Maggie on the occasions when she won't cooperate. Doug has to hold her while Prudence brushes her teeth. But they remain calm and loving throughout. It goes something like this: "We know you don't like this process, but toothbrushing is a have-to. It is our job as your mommy and daddy to be sure your whole body is strong and healthy. We are happy to be helpers until you are ready to do it on your own." While this is uncomfortable for everyone, after following through on this plan just two times, Maggie stops resisting and cooperates with brushing her teeth.

There are now many mornings when Maggie has completed her tasks in the time allotted so she gets to do the math game with Doug. And, with these mindshifts and new approaches to helping Maggie get through daily routines—sticking to limits while remaining calm and loving—Doug and Prudence are able to apply similar strategies throughout the day that result in a major reduction in power struggles overall.

SEBASTIAN AND TALIA: BEDTIME BEDLAM

Audrey and Stephen have two children, Talia and Sebastian, ages five and three. They fight all day long. But, at bedtime, they miraculously morph into the best of buddies. They share a room and create total chaos together just when it is time for lights-out. They start jumping on beds, throwing pillows, and getting super revved up at just the time that Audrey and Stephen want them to settle down. This is making bedtime incredibly stressful. Audrey and Stephen end up doing a lot of shouting and threatening, which only riles up the kids more. They ultimately throw up their hands. They don't know how to get Sebastian and Talia to settle down and go to sleep.

Mindsets and Mindshifts

Like Doug and Prudence, Audrey and Stephen are stuck in the mindset that *they need to and can control their children's behavior and get them to cooperate.* When we examine the dynamics at play, outside the heat of the moment, it becomes clear to them that *focusing on trying to force Talia and Sebastian to change their behavior is not helping Audrey and Stephen gain control over the situation.* This mindshift motivates them to come up with a plan that they have the ability to enforce and puts them in control of bedtime.

The Plan

Audrey and Stephen move from being reactive to responsive. They love that the kids have such a good time together before bedtime and want to encourage that, so they bake into their new plan an opportunity for this rough-and-tumble kind of play. After books and before lights-out, they institute a 10-minute period they call "sibling silly time" when Talia and Sebastian can play on their own in their room. Then, Audrey or Stephen returns to tuck them in and say good night. At that point, the direction is for Talia and Sebastian to calm their minds and bodies to sleep. This means staying in their own beds and no more noise.

They get clear on what they can and can't control in this situation. They state outright to the kids: "It is your voice and your bodies. Only you have control over what you say and what you do. We can't make you be quiet or stay in your beds after lights-out, but, to be sure you get the sleep you need to be healthy and strong, we are going to establish some rules. If you choose to keep talking and getting out of bed after lights-out, we will separate you. One of you will go to sleep in Mom and Dad's room. (Audrey and Stephen place a mattress in the corner of their bedroom and make a cozy corner where a child can sleep if necessary.) The other will stay in your bedroom. When we go to sleep, we will move whoever falls asleep in our room back to his or her own bed. We will create a calendar to track whose turn it is to sleep in our room." While Audrey and Stephen don't love the idea of having a child fall asleep in their bedroom, given the reality of the space in their home, they see this as a loving plan that they can feel good about. Most importantly, it's a plan that they have control over implementing—that doesn't depend on the kids' cooperation.

They avoid playing referee with the kids. They make it clear to Talia and Sebastian that, if there is noise or movement after lights-out, they will not get involved in who started it. They will just implement the plan. (This is a very important feature of a successful plan. Otherwise, you risk going down the "he said, she said" rabbit hole, which is hard to untangle and can completely divert you from setting a clear, effective limit.)

The Outcome

On the first night, the kids completely ignore the plan. As soon as the lights go out, they are up and at it again. Audrey refrains from going into the gray zone of trying to coax the kids to calm down and go to sleep, as familiar and tempting as that is. She simply tells Talia that it is her turn to go to mommy and daddy's bed to sleep. Talia resists. Audrey tells Talia that she has two great choices, either she can walk on her own to the other bedroom or Audrey will be a helper and carry her. Talia giggles and hides under the covers. With as much calm as she can muster, Audrey picks up Talia and carries her to the parental bedroom. She has to use a gadget that prevents Talia from being able to open the bedroom door and keep running back to her own bedroom. (See the appendix for a list of these kinds of gadgets.)

On the second night, Audrey and Stephen make a point of reminding the kids about their choices: staying quiet after lights out means they get to stay in the room together; making noise means someone gets moved. They also add a one-minute warning (visualized with a timer) before sibling silly time ends. And when they go in to say good night and turn the lights off, they give the kids one minute to think about what choice they are going to make about being quiet.

Over the course of the next week, there are a few nights when the kids don't follow the rule and one child has to go into Mom and Dad's room. By the second week, there is a significant reduction in these occurrences. And even when the kids are too excited to follow the rules, now that Audrey and Stephen have a firm, reasonable plan that they have been able to implement calmly and lovingly, they feel back in control and no longer dread bedtime.

OLIVER: THE LITTLE NONLISTENER

Mandy and Dev complain that Oliver, their three-year-old, just won't listen (aka cooperate). They have to ask him three or four times to do something—to put away his toys, wash his hands before a meal, or stop an activity that is dangerous (such as catapulting himself off the bed or throwing the driveway gravel). This defiance has gotten worse since his baby sister was born a few months ago. Mandy and Dev are getting increasingly frustrated with having to nag him and raise their voices all the time. When they yell, Oliver starts to cry and one or both of them gives in and ends up caving on the limit. Oliver goes to the table with dirty hands. Dad ends up cleaning up the toys. Or they find themselves resorting to bribery—a tactic they had secretly criticized other parents for using before they had kids themselves. (Those in glass houses . . .) They offer extra screen time if he will stop jumping off the bed or tossing the gravel.

They feel terrible about having such negative feelings toward their child, whom they love so deeply. With significant sadness, Mandy concludes: "We are reduced to bribery-based parenting. We don't know what else to do."

The Mindsets and Mindshifts

As we take a step back to reflect on the dynamic at play, Mandy and Dev see that their anger at Oliver is due to the fact that he is making them feel out of control, like incompetent parents who cannot make their child behave. Their efforts to get him to follow basic rules and expectations are backfiring. He is driving the car and taking them for a ride. Once they see *that it is their focus on trying to get Oliver to change his behavior that results in this dynamic, they are open to thinking about other ways to engage Oliver's cooperation that keep them in the driver's seat while giving Oliver some control that he so desperately craves.*

Replaying typical encounters with Oliver, Mandy and Dev also become aware that they are constantly asking for Oliver's agreement when it comes to making a transition or imposing a limit. They pervasively pose directions as questions, for example, "No jumping on the bed, *okay*?" or "Would you like to clean up?" They realize that they are doing this to compensate for the fact that Oliver is having a hard time adjusting to the new baby. They are concerned about stressing him out more, so they find themselves tiptoeing around him. *They fear giving him a direction will set him off, so they unconsciously frame their expectations as questions—inadvertently communicating that they are asking for his buy-in.* They are hoping against hope that Oliver will get with the program so they can all happily move on. But they see that this approach is backfiring and ultimately causing them, and Oliver, more stress as the situation devolves into an ugly power struggle. *With this insight, Mandy and Dev start to get comfortable with being the loving authority figures Oliver needs them to be.* (Kids have parents for a reason. Being a strong, loving leader is in your job description!)

The Plan

They validate Oliver's experience and show empathy. They acknowledge that having to share attention with his sister is a big change and that it will take time to adapt to having a sibling. Taking this empathetic approach makes them feel better about setting and sticking to expectations and limits with Oliver. It's not love or limits; it's love *and* limits.

They stop using rewards/bribery and threats to get Oliver to cooperate.

They teach Oliver the difference between a choice and a direction. A choice is something he gets to pick, such as whether he wants a yogurt or apple slices for snack. A direction is something that has to be done, such as the TV being turned off after his show is over. They also stop communicating directions as questions. There's no more saying "Time to clean up the toys, *okay*?" Instead, they say, "It's time to clean up. Do you want to put the trucks or the blocks away first?"

They make a plan for how to secure Oliver's attention. When it's time to give Oliver a direction, they call his name once. If he doesn't respond, they place their hand on his right shoulder and say "pause." This signals to him that it's time to stop what he is doing and listen. If he is still having a hard time tuning in to them, they help him by removing the distraction (or "brain teaser" as my occupational therapist colleagues call them). For example, if Oliver is bouncing a ball and doesn't put it down when they are trying to communicate with him, they respond lightheartedly: "I see a brain teaser! I'm going to be a helper and put the ball away so you can focus your attention on what I need to tell you. You can play with the ball again after naptime." (Notice how all the directions are positive, not threatening. There is no "If you don't put that ball down right now, I am going to take it, and you won't get it back for a week.")

They provide warnings before transitions. They use a visual timer to show Oliver how much time he has before an upcoming transition. They help him think about how he wants to spend the last few minutes of the activity he is engaged in to give him a sense of control.

They institute a new system to prevent their own reactivity and be more effective at that inevitable moment when Oliver is not cooperating with a direction. They state the problem very matter-of-factly: "We see you are having a hard time following the direction to stop throwing gravel." Then, they explain: "Mommy and daddy are going to have a short meeting to think about how we can help you follow this direction." (At this point, I have seen many kids stop in their tracks and comply with the request, so shocked are they at their parents' lack of reactivity and unexpected, calm response.) This gives Mandy and Dev a minute to think through what choices they can offer Oliver that will lead to an end to his throwing gravel—whether or not he chooses to comply—so that they remain in control of the situation and avoid resorting to bribery and threats. In this case, they come up with "The gravel cannot be thrown. It's unsafe. You have two great choices, either you can put the gravel down and we can help you find something safe to toss, or we can help you come inside to prevent you from throwing the stones. You decide." This strategy serves many important purposes: it prevents Mandy and Dev from being reactive—giving them time to think clearly about the situation at hand, which also serves as a great role model for Oliver about managing emotions; collaborating on a response shows Oliver that they are a team, working together to be his helpers and also reduces the chance they will undermine each other with differing reactions to Oliver's behavior; and it emphasizes to Oliver that he has choices; he is the decider of the outcome—whether he gets to stay outside and play or goes inside.

The Outcome

As expected, Oliver becomes more defiant when they start the new plan. (Even minor changes to the rules of engagement can lead to major protests. Kids get comfortable with the existing system and will fight, some more fiercely than others, to reinstate it. It takes time for them to adapt to the new program.) He comes on strong with threats and vitriol to the tune of "I will not put the blocks away. They are *your* blocks, not my blocks!" And then there is this doozy of a response when they tell him it's time to put the tablet away: "If you say that to me again, I am going to take your voice box and throw it in the garbage." Mandy and Dev know not to react to these pronouncements at face value. They respond by acknowledging that he doesn't like the limit they are setting and that is fine. They are not asking him to agree with it, but they are still going to enforce it because that is their job.

As frequently happens, Oliver rejects the choices they offer: "Those are bad choices! I will tell you the choices!" But when Mandy and Dev refrain from getting reactive and follow through with the plan, they start to see progress. The most powerful element turns out to be the mommy/daddy meeting: giving themselves time to pause and problem solve. It is especially effective when they discuss the issue at hand aloud, in front of Oliver. He is totally tuned in to their dialogue about what choices they are going to give him and is much more likely to cooperate when they employ this strategy.

By the end of the second week, there is a sizable decrease in defiance and a major increase in cooperation. There are, of course, times when Oliver still chooses not to comply with a direction or make a good choice; for example, he continues to play with the gravel, instead of accepting an alternative, and has to go inside. He may have a meltdown when they implement the limit, but Mandy and Dev have gotten comfortable with that, allowing Oliver to have his upset instead of trying to make it all better. Most importantly, there are no more battles, and Mandy and Dev are no longer exhausted or consumed with anger and frustration at Oliver. They are back in control in a way that feels loving and positive. They don't have to fear the tantrum or the power struggle. What a huge relief!

SADIE: BREAKFAST BATTLES

Adam and Brian are entrenched in breakfast battles with Sadie, their three-year-old. While she enjoys and will eat a range of foods when she wants to, she lollygags and gets up and down from the table for a seemingly endless array of urgent tasks she insists must be undertaken. She keeps going back to her room to make sure her teddy's blanket is still on securely. She searches for the toy she wants to bring to school. Her dads vacillate between trying to convince her to eat—telling her she will be hungry at school—and making threats, such as no treat after school if she doesn't stay at the table. None of these tactics motivates Sadie to sit and eat. When they announce that it's time to leave for school after the more-than-adequate 20 minutes they have allotted for breakfast, Sadie has barely taken three small bites of her toast. She starts shouting: "You didn't give me any time to eat! You can't take away my food!" Exasperated, but worried that she will be hungry at school, Adam and Brian give her five more minutes, which turns into 10 and then 15. Still, she only nibbles and continues to get up and down from the table. They finally, angrily, pick her up and get her into her car seat, scolding her for making everyone late. Sadie, in hysterics, shouts that they are meanies for taking her food away. She is going to tell the teacher on them and is going to be mad all day! They respond by lecturing her all the way to school about how it is her fault if she doesn't eat. Everyone is miserable.

The Mindsets and Mindshifts

In taking a step back to look objectively at this dynamic, Adam and Brian are able to see that their focus on *trying to get Sadie to change her behavior is failing because Sadie is not swayed by the range of tactics they employ.* The situation is maddening because she is in control of how their morning routine goes—and it's not going well.

It's further complicated by *Sadie's vitriol and threats that they are taking at face value. Her proclamation that she is going to be mad all day is triggering to Adam and Brian.* They have visions of her being mean to her friends and noncompliant with her teachers if she is cranky at school because she hasn't eaten. This makes them worry about setting limits in the morning that put her in a bad mood for the rest of the day.

The important mindshift they make is that Sadie is just a very clever three-year-old who knows their triggers and is using threats to get them to change their minds—a proven strategy. *She doesn't mean exactly what she says.* In fact, Sadie's teachers report that she is always a good friend and has no history of social challenges. The struggles they have at home do not extend to her behavior in the outside world. *Sadie is simply being strategic, not manipulative. Her system to get what she wants is working on them so she is sticking with it.*

The final hurdle Adam and Brian have to overcome is the mindset that *it is "mean" to set limits around mealtimes and restrict Sadie's access to food.* It feels terrible to refuse her food when she says she's hungry, regardless of the fact that they have given her plenty of time to eat. Once we peel back the layers and assess the situation objectively, Adam and Brian are able to make the mindshift *that it is the lack of limits around mealtime that is reducing Sadie's food intake and increasing the battles, which results in their acting "mean"—exactly what they are trying to avoid. This insight motivates Adam and Brian to get comfortable with setting clear limits around breakfast.* They see that boundaries are not restrictive (the negative attribution that had been hampering them) but instead are helpful. They will provide the structure to enable Sadie to make better choices around mealtime and reduce the power struggles that are harmful to all of them.

The Plan

They set clear limits around breakfast. They use a visual timer and make it clear that, when the timer beeps, breakfast is over. The food will be put away at that point.

They give Sadie a sense of control. They acknowledge to Sadie that it is her body and only she can decide what she eats. She knows what her belly needs. If it gets filled up, it's happy and feels good. If she chooses not to fill her belly, it may be unhappy and growl. They then explain that she has two great choices at breakfast: either she can come to the table and fill her belly with what it needs to feel satisfied and give her the energy she needs, or she can choose not to come to the table and not to fill her belly before time is up. In that case, she can put her remaining breakfast in a container to take with her so she can eat it on the way to school in case she gets hungry.

This plan feels fair and appropriate to Adam and Brian. It gets them out of the business of trying to control Sadie's behavior and sets her up to make good choices for herself.

The Outcome

The first morning they implement this plan, not surprisingly, Sadie tests it. She runs back and forth from the table and keeps bidding for their attention—asking for help to get a toy from the shelf and other assorted requests that she is accustomed to having her dads fulfill. Adam and Brian stay put at the table. They remind Sadie that their attention now is on breakfast and they will stay there until the timer goes off and they have filled their bellies. They will be happy to help her once breakfast is over. They make a point of letting her know that they would love for her to join them at the table when she's ready—they miss having great mealtime conversations with her.

When Sadie sees that her dads are sticking to the limits they set, she finally sits down at the table and starts eating—just five minutes before time is up. When the timer goes off, it takes every ounce of self-control Adam and Brian have not to let Sadie keep eating. But they stick to the plan, much to Sadie's disbelief. As they start to move the food away and ask Sadie if she'd like to choose a container in which to put the food she hadn't had time to eat, she starts screaming that she will not put any food in any container and that she will just starve all day. Adam and Brian stay the course while remaining calm and loving. They tell Sadie that they understand that her belly isn't full because she chose to play rather than come to the table. But the good news is that she can make a different decision tomorrow at breakfast and eat what her belly needs to feel satisfied.

They then ask Sadie whether she wants to take the food to go. They tell her that, because this is a really big decision to make, they will give her a whole minute to think about it and give them her answer. In the meantime, they busy themselves with cleaning up and ignore her continued protestations. When the minute is up, Sadie pronounces that she will NEVER take the food to go and that they are the meanest daddies on earth. Adam and Brian do not get reactive in the face of her threats and vitriol. They remind themselves that this is just a three-year-old's way of expressing how unhappy she is with their rule; and that just because Sadie doesn't like a limit doesn't mean it's not good for her.

Sadie continues to stomp around and refuses to cooperate with getting into the car seat to go to school. They acknowledge that she is having a hard time and they are happy to be her helpers. Adam and Brian put her into the car seat. They ignore her kicking and screaming but stay connected by putting on Sadie's favorite songs and belting out the lyrics in the funny way that she likes as they drive her to school. As expected, they are worried about how she will do in the classroom after this challenging morning. The teacher keeps them posted. At 11:00 a.m., they receive a text reporting that Sadie is having a great day and that she ate a lot at snack time.

By the third morning of implementing the new system, breakfast battles are mostly bygones.

STRATEGIES FOR ENCOURAGING COOPERATION

Make a visual schedule. This provides a concrete tool to guide your child through each step of your morning and evening routine. It can be very effective for easing transitions. Include your child in creating the schedule. Take photos of all your child's daily routines, for example, waking up in the morning, having breakfast, getting dressed, brushing teeth, and getting into the car or bus.

Be sure to include the people who participate in or help with these routines (caregivers and grandparents) so the photos reflect your child's reality. Take photos of mom helping with getting dressed in the morning and dad giving a hug at preschool drop-off. Then, help your child create the calendar, providing whatever support she needs based on her age and ability. You might even have her choose what she will eat for breakfast the night before (like we did with Maggie) and include it on the schedule. This can reduce challenges in the morning.

Go through the same process for the evening and nighttime routines. Take photos of every important step of the process. You can create the calendar for the evening routine at the time you feel would work best for your child. Some families do it during breakfast for kids who fiercely depend on predictability and like to know exactly what is coming down the pike. For some children, this is too much to process in the morning; in that case, it works better to create a ritual of doing a brief family meeting before dinner to go over what the plan will be for the whole evening, for example, dinner, bath, brushing teeth, books, and bed. Again, be sure to take photos of all the people who might be involved in these routines so your child knows exactly what to expect, such as daddy is doing bath tonight, and papa is reading the books.

It can be helpful to provide a way for your child to note that he has completed a task. He might put a check mark or a sticker next to each photo as he moves through the routine. The more actively involved your child is in the process, the more likely he is to cooperate.

Teach your child the difference between a direction and a choice. Remember, when you are giving your child a direction, you are not asking for his agreement or buy-in. This does not mean you are being a dictator! Children *want to know exactly what is expected* of them. Good teachers are masterful at being loving while also making expectations very clear.

Direct, don't correct. Children, especially those who are highly sensitive and reactive by nature, tend to feel shamed and overwhelmed when being corrected. When they hear "no," their brains become flooded with emotion and they are unable to think or problem solve. This makes it much less likely they will comply and change their behavior in positive ways.

So, skip the "no" and provide a clear direction about the expectation and what your child *can* do. For example, if your child goes for a toy when you've told her it's time to get pj's on, instead of saying "It's not playing time; put that down and get your pajamas on," you simply say "We're putting on pajamas now" as you guide her away from the toy.

This approach also has an added benefit: it entails a lot less language than we tend to use when we are frustrated and trying to get our children to cooperate. We give a long lecture thinking we can convince our children to do the right thing. But this tends to have the opposite effect. When a limit is being set, it's stressful for kids. They have to stop doing something they enjoy in order to comply with someone else's agenda. The more we talk, the more agitated and overstimulated children become, which escalates their frustration and interferes with their ability to self-regulate and comply. This positive and to-the-point strategy also helps *you* self-regulate. All that lecturing tends to increase parents' emotional intensity. Providing clear direction is simpler, keeps everybody calmer, and makes you more effective at setting limits.

Give your child a sense of control over the transition. "It's time to get into the car. Do you want to bring a book or listen to an audiobook?" "It's time to go upstairs for bath. Do you want to hop like a bunny or slither up the stairs like a snake? Which will it be?" The more your child feels he has some control over the process, the more likely he will be to cooperate.

Use the concept of "first, then" to let your child know when she will be able to do the activity she desires. This is a handy strategy to use when your child is angling to do an activity that can't happen at that moment: "I know you want to play with the balls. Great idea! First, we need to clean up these toys, and then we can play with the balls." "You are so eager to ride your bike. It's so much fun. First, nap, and then bike." When you acknowledge your child's desire and confirm that she will be able to do what she wants at some later point, you reduce the stress she typically experiences when she can't get what she wants right away. This reassurance can be calming and can put her in a more positive frame of mind. This may make her more willing to comply.

Provide a warning to help your child anticipate a transition. As you know by now, I am a big fan of visual timers because they help children track how much time they have left to finish what they are doing before they have to make a change. They can be used for many purposes, including showing your child how much time he has for books before bed; how much time he has for screen use or any other activity; or how much time he has to complete a task, such as cleaning up or getting dressed. Be sure to place the timer out of your child's reach. Clever kids have been known to adjust the time to their benefit.

Beware the brain teaser. These are distractions that call your child's attention away from what you want him to be focusing on. In these moments, you might say "Oh, brain teaser!" as you point to the distraction, which might be another book on the shelf or a toy he is reaching for when you have asked him to wash his hands before snack. Then, add "It's time to turn your brain off of your toy and onto hand-washing."

Another typical scenario is when you've directed your child to retrieve a specific object, such as his shoes, and along the way he sees a ball and starts to play with it. In this situation, you might say "Oops, brain teaser. What was your job?" This provides a cue to get him back on track in a positive way, without nagging.

If your child is still having trouble following through on the direction, for example, to put the ball away, let him know you will be his helper: "Oh, bud, do you need a helper? I'm going to count to three to give you time to decide whether you will put the ball down and come get your shoes on or if I need to be a helper and put it away." If he doesn't comply after the count of three, you take the ball and put it in the "wait space"—essentially anywhere your child can't access the object. This takes the distraction out of the equation and helps your child focus on the task at hand.

Establish a cue with your child to signal that you want his attention. For example, firmly placing your hand on your child's shoulder (the tactic Oliver's parents used so effectively). The more ritualized these cues become, the more effective they are. Think of all the cuing that goes on in group settings to help children with transitions: singing a song to signal that it's cleanup time or ringing a bell when it's time to line up to go outside. These are tools that help kids know what to expect and can lead to greater cooperation.

Teach your child to pause. This is another strategy for helping your child stop what he is doing and pay attention. Explain to your child that, when you stretch out your arm and hold up your hand as you say pause, it is time for her to stop what she's doing and get her mind and body ready to listen. (Of course, you can make up whatever cue you like. For example, in many preschools, they say "1, 2, 3, eyes on me.")

You can say "pause" to cue your child to tune in when more typical strategies for getting her attention, such as calling her name or telling her you have a question to ask her, haven't worked. (When we call children's names over and over, they tend to tune it out; think Charlie Brown's teacher.) If your child is still not tuning in to you, you can place your hand over the object your child is focused on to provide additional support for turning off his brain from whatever is distracting him and turning it onto what you need to communicate to him.

Use the concept of "two great choices" (also known as the "choice of no choices") when your child is decidedly not cooperating. Say that the direction to your child was to stop playing and take a bath. You gave him the choice to hop like a bunny or slither like a snake up the stairs to help him make the transition. He ignores the choices or outright defies the direction. This is the moment when you need to pause to ask yourself what you do and don't control in the situation at hand. In this case, what you decidedly *don't* control is the ability to *make* your child climb up the stairs. You need to have a plan with an outcome you control, which means it can't depend on waiting for your child to comply. That's when employing two great choices can be very effective. "Charlie, you have two great choices: either you can go upstairs on your own, or I will carry you up. You decide." "Marin, it is time to give the big truck to your brother for his turn. You have two great choices: either you can give it back, or I will be a helper and give it to him. You decide." This approach enables you to stay in control of the situation. Focusing on the fact that your child is the decider and you are just implementing the consequences of his choices also makes children feel more in control and less defiant.

Many parents worry that this is somehow giving in to their child, for example, carrying him up the stairs instead of making him walk on his own. Philosophically, that makes a lot of sense. But theory doesn't always work in practice. You have to ask yourself what the alternative is. Waiting for your child to comply puts him in the driver's seat for how the situation will go. This dynamic is not healthy for you or your child and results in a lot of unpleasant battles. Rest assured, once you follow through on limits like these a few times, your child will be hopping or slithering up the stairs on his own.

Avoid threats. Your tone is infectious. When you get revved up and this kind of thing comes rolling off your tongue, "If you don't put the crayons down on the count of three, you won't have them for a week!," it puts your child in a more defiant posture, making it less likely that she will cooperate. Instead, try "You have two great choices: you can either follow the direction to put the crayons away, or I will be a helper and put them away so you can focus on eating your breakfast."

Use natural consequences in lieu of rewards. I am not a fan of rewards. They send a message to children that whatever accomplishment they have achieved is valid or valued only if it results in some kind of external reinforcer, like more sweets or extra screen time. What I think we really want for our kids is for the prize to be the internal sense of satisfaction they get from gaining more independence or achieving a new skill. In addition, using rewards often results in children becoming dependent on them, demanding a prize for everything. You tell them it's time to clean up or to get dressed, and they ask what they will get as a reward.

I am a big fan of natural consequences, such as linking cooperation with having more or less time for fun activities because this reflects the natural consequences we all experience in the real world. If we spend an hour playing solitaire on the computer during our workday, we won't have time to meet a friend for lunch, or we may have to work into the evening. If your child cooperates with getting into the car seat after school, she will have extra time to play at home. If she chooses not to cooperate, no problem; you will be a helper and get her into the car, but there won't be extra time for play. You are not taking anything away, nor is this punishment. It is just the way life works.

For the bedtime routine, you might use the visual timer to show your child how much time there is until lights out. The sooner he puts on his pajamas and brushes his teeth, the more time he'll have for books.

You can also use the incentive of banking time. You allot a specific amount of time for each task. If your child cooperates with a task in less time than is allotted, such as getting dressed in under 10 minutes, he can bank that time for use in a desired activity later. You can make it into a math activity and, together with your child, add up the time he has saved. Then, he gets to choose—from acceptable options you offer—how to spend the banked time. It might mean getting to read a book with you before heading to school or extra playtime before bed. This can serve as a powerful incentive. It is also a great alternative to using rewards or negative consequences, which often have no connection to the actual incident, can be shaming, and tend to backfire.

Take a parental pause to problem solve. When you are in reactive mode, it is very hard to think clearly and plan your response. To help parents with this perennial challenge, I have come up with a simple strategy to prevent reactivity: taking a "mommy/daddy moment" to give yourself a chance to think about how to respond in a way that leads to greater cooperation from your children that is calm and loving, not harsh or threatening.

Just as Mandy and Dev enacted with Oliver, you can take the following steps when your child is not cooperating with a direction: (1) State the problem: "Fiona, I see you are having a hard time following the direction to get your backpack from your cubby so we can get into the car to go home." (2) Explain that you are going to take a mommy/daddy moment to think about how you can help your child make this transition. If you are by yourself, tap your head as you think aloud about what choices you can give your child that will solve the problem. This can be very instructive and entertaining for kids. "Hmm, let's see. Fiona is having a hard time following through on the direction to get her backpack. I can see how it might be hard to leave school, which she loves, and make the change to go home. That makes sense. But we need to get home for dinner and to have time to play before bed. So how can I help Fiona solve this problem? I can't make her get her backpack—only she can decide to do that. So I guess her two great choices can be to get her backpack and go to the car on her own, or I will grab the backpack and help Fiona to the car so we can get home to make dinner. If Fiona chooses to cooperate, that will mean extra time to play before dinner. If I need to get the backpack and take her to the car, that will take more time so we won't have extra playtime before dinner. I will have to get right to cooking." Then, you turn to your child and reiterate what she's just overheard you brainstorm, ostensibly to yourself, and emphasize that the outcome is in her hands. She decides which option it will be. You will just implement the outcome of her choice.

This approach can be very powerful to enact with your spouse/partner. "It looks like Martin is having trouble following the direction to come inside for nap. Let's take a mommy/daddy moment to figure out how we can help solve this problem." Per the example above, it can be very effective to have this discussion in front of your child (if you can do it calmly and respectfully). It shows your child that you and your partner are working together to support him and prevents you and your partner from undermining each other ("But daddy said I could do it!").

FINAL THOUGHTS

The definition of cooperation is, "An act or instance of working or acting together for a shared purpose or benefit."[7] When you provide clear directions and choices, you are helping your child work toward the common good—for both you and him.

3

TANTRUMS

Luisa gives Mateo, her four-year-old, a five-minute warning to prepare him that screen time will be ending soon. He ignores her and keeps his eyes glued to the tablet. When the timer goes off, Luisa asks Mateo to give her the device. Mateo shouts that he's not done. Luisa reminds Mateo that he got a warning and that he knows the rule: when the timer goes off, the tablet goes away. She asks him several more times to give it up but ultimately has to pry it out of his hands. He throws himself to the ground and bats his hands and kicks his feet at her when she tries to comfort him. Luisa, becoming increasingly agitated, tells him he has to take a time-out, but Mateo refuses to go to the stairs where he is supposed to sit. He shouts that her rules are dumb and that she is a mean mommy. Luisa storms away, shouting back at Mateo, "Don't you dare talk to me that way! You are impossible!" Mateo chases after her, sobbing, "Mama, mama, mama!" Luisa's tears also start to flow, and she responds, "Mama wouldn't get mad if you just followed the rule without a fuss. You are making mama so sad. If you calm down, I will give you a few more minutes with the tablet." He pulls it together, and she gives him the tablet.

A similar scenario is repeated week after week, and the conflicts are not limited to issues around the tablet. Almost every time Luisa doesn't give Mateo exactly what he wants, he melts down. This makes her feel constantly on edge, like she is walking on eggshells, dreading the next limit she needs to impose that will set Mateo off. She stops limiting tablet time and caves on a lot of her other rules—like letting him eat more snack foods than she thinks is healthy for him or staying up later than she knows is good for him—just to avoid these unpleasant interactions, especially when they take place in public.

Most young children throw tantrums at one point or another—some more than others. In thirty-three years of working with families, I have yet to meet a young child who never melted down in the face of life's inevitable challenges. Some of these tantrums are expected, like when they are in response to your saying no to a cookie before dinner or to staying longer at the playground. At other times, they seem completely irrational, like when your child flips out because you put the chicken too close to the noodles on her plate or pushed the elevator button when she wanted to do it (but neglected to tell you). In these moments, many parents wonder how they have raised a "spoiled" child who holds them hostage with her irrational demands and meltdowns as soon as she doesn't get something she believes she desperately needs. Parents catastrophize, an occupational hazard, worrying how their child is ever going to make it in life if she can't handle these seemingly minor upsets.

The good news is, there is nothing wrong with your child. She is not spoiled or ungrateful. She is not purposefully trying to drive you insane or make you look like a terrible parent. Like Mateo, your child is just having a hard time managing her strong feelings of frustration, anger, and disappointment, which is totally normal for a young child.

When I guide parents in reflecting on the tantrums and what gets triggered for them in these moments, several faulty mindsets consistently emerge that present obstacles to their handling tantrums in a way that is both loving and effective, and results in an overall reduction in their children's meltdowns.

My child should be able to accept limits and exhibit greater self-control. When I ask parents about their expectations of their children, they almost always believe that their kids should be able to exert much greater self-control than they are actually capable of. The mindshift to make is that your child is not losing it on purpose. Remember, the part of the brain that helps us think about our feelings and make a plan for how to deal with them—the "upstairs brain"—is in the very early stages of development in kids five and under. Even then, this ability for self-regulation remains a work in progress for most of us well into adulthood.[8] The distress at not getting something they want triggers their reactive "downstairs brain," which results in their acting on their feelings, no matter how many times you plead with them to use their words. Even when a child can talk about her feelings (which is still very limited in two- and three-year-olds), young children are much more likely to express their emotions through their actions. They need patience and support to learn to manage their big emotions, also known as self-regulation.

When establishing expectations for your child's ability to self-regulate, it's also important to consider your child's temperament. Those children who are highly sensitive (HS) by nature tend to have a harder time managing their emotions because they process their experiences in the world more intensely. Their threshold for stress is lower than those go-with-the-flow "dandelions" who have a higher tolerance for typical life challenges, such as making transitions and not getting something they want. These easygoing kids, by nature, tend to be more flexible and thus better able to manage life's ups and downs, while HS children are often bigger reactors who lose it more frequently and often with more fervor. For kids who are HS, like Mateo, seemingly minor stressors can result in major meltdowns. If you have an intense, sensitive, fierce little one, these kinds of upsets are to be expected.

Context is also an important variable that affects children's ability to cope with life's frustrations and disappointments. A major change in their world, such as a new baby, a move, a loss . . . or a pandemic (which is raging as I write this book), can result in more frequent and intense tantrums. When children are dealing with a seismic shift in their daily lives, their brains and bodies go into survival mode. This means they have less emotional energy for the higher-functioning capacity for self-regulation.[9]

It is mean and rejecting to not give my child what she says she wants and needs. Often, what triggers a child into a tantrum is your having set some kind of limit she doesn't like; for example, having to leave a friend's home, not getting a toy at the store, or not letting her climb onto the stair banister. The list is endless. Parents report that, during these meltdowns, they often feel that not giving their children what they want is harmful to them; that ending an activity they love, like leaving the playground or not telling them another story before bedtime, is being mean and rejecting. This feeling is amplified when their children react with proclamations that pull on heartstrings, like "You're not being a kind daddy," "You don't love me," or "I never get enough stories."

Parents will do a lot of mental gymnastics to rationalize why it's okay to give in to their children's demands to prevent or end the tantrum. This mindset is directly connected to the next.

Tantrums are harmful to my child. Many parents feel that it is detrimental for their children to be in a state of distress, especially the moms and dads of kids who are feisty and fierce. One of these dads described his daughter's shrieking when she doesn't get her way as "slaughterhouse screams." It's hard not to get triggered in these moments and to try to do everything you can to prevent them from happening in the first place or to just make the tantrums stop once they've started. But this mindset results in parents backing off of limits that they know are good for their child—like sticking to a bedtime routine—to avoid a meltdown.

So it's important to make the mindshift that *tantrums in and of themselves are not harmful to children.* Remember, the distress children experience when they can't get something they want is *manageable stress* that leads to the ability to self-regulate and be resilient in the face of life's challenges. Difficult feelings are not harmful to children. They are a part of life. Your job isn't to take them away but to trust that your child can learn to manage the challenges she faces, with your help.

I can control my child and make her change her behavior. Once the tantrum begins, most parents engage in a range of strategies to get their child to pull herself together. They try to talk her out of her upset: "It's okay; you'll get to go back to the playground tomorrow." They make threats: "If you don't stop screaming and crying you won't get any screen time tomorrow." They offer rewards: "You can get a special treat before bedtime if you calm down." While some of these strategies work some of the time, they can have an unintended negative consequence: when you make it all better or threaten your child out of his upset, it is a missed opportunity for him to learn to manage his difficult feelings and see that he can cope with the challenges he faces.

But, more often than not, I find that these strategies backfire. When children are triggered into stress mode, they lose control of their minds and bodies.[10] In this "red zone,"[11] the brain is flooded with emotion. They have no bandwidth to process any information. The more you try to talk your child out of his upset, the more agitated he becomes—escalating the tantrum.

The critical shift in mindset is that *you cannot make your child calm down*. What you can do is respond in a way that makes it more likely she will be able to calm herself. Your reaction has a lot of power; it can either help calm your child or escalate the meltdown. While I know it can be hard to feel, and act, with love and empathy in the face of an epic, irrational meltdown, this seemingly impossible goal is within your reach. I'm not saying this is easy; learning to manage your own reactions when you get triggered by your children's irrational behavior takes a lot of motivation and mindfulness. But it is worth the effort because the payoff is huge, for both you and your child. These changes in mindset should help.

Tantrums are (relatively!) short-lived stressors in service of long-term goals. When you are able to see the tantrum as temporary distress that leads to the development of strong coping skills and resilience in the long term, you will no longer live in fear of the tantrum.

The stories and solutions described in this chapter illustrate how changes in your mindset can free you to be present for your child when she is struggling—to show her that she is seen and not alone—while sticking to limits that help your child build confidence in her ability to work through difficult experiences.

MATEO: SCREEN-TIME BATTLES

Thinking back to Luisa and Mateo's epic tablet battles, there are several mindsets at play that are making it hard for Luisa to set and enforce the limits that are important for Mateo's development.

The Mindsets and Mindshifts

It all begins with Luisa's worry *that Mateo's state of distress when he doesn't get what he wants is harmful to him*. This mindset results in her abdicating on limits that she knows in her head are important for Mateo but that don't feel right in her heart. Once she understands that *the distress of not getting something he wants does not have long-term, negative consequences and that giving in to Mateo is actually resulting in an increase, not a decrease, in tantrums*, Luisa feels more comfortable with the idea of sticking to important limits.

Along these lines, Luisa is also able to see that *her focus on trying to get Mateo to change his behavior (to agree with her plan and hand over the tablet when time is up or to sit in time-out) isn't effective because she has no control over whether Mateo will comply with her directions.* She can't make him hand over the tablet or sit still on the stairs. Mateo can keep getting up, which will only further infuriate her and intensify her feeling of being out of control of the situation. When Luisa sees that there is nothing wrong with Mateo, that her approach is the problem, she feels empowered to make a positive change. She is relieved that there is something *she* can do to help Mateo learn to accept and follow rules and to effect an important change in her relationship with Mateo overall.

It also comes as a relief to Luisa that *Mateo's angry and provocative statements are to be expected and don't signal that he is a "bad" kid.* (Think about all the venom that comes out of adults' mouths when we are triggered!) Making the mindshift that *Mateo doesn't mean exactly what he says, that he is just a three-year-old venting his anger and frustration in the only way he knows how,* reduces her reactivity. Luisa sees that responding to his vitriol at face value, as if he is purposefully trying to hurt her, only escalates the situation. (This is one of those counterintuitive phenomena; you think that telling your child that he is hurting your feelings or making you sad will motivate him to change his behavior. But the idea that he could hurt you is overwhelming and confusing to your child; he doesn't mean his statements in the way you are interpreting them. When you have a big, angry reaction, he gets flooded with emotion and is less likely to calm down and learn any lessons from the experience. It is much more effective to approach these moments matter-of-factly and address the underlying feeling your child is expressing: "I know you are mad at mommy for taking away the tablet. It's okay to be mad at me, but I am still going to limit screen time. That is my job.")

The Plan

Luisa makes the expectations clear. "You will have 30 minutes on the tablet."

She shows empathy for Mateo's experience and doesn't try to control or minimize his emotions. It goes something like this: "I know you don't like it when screen time is over. I completely understand. Why would you want to stop doing something you are really enjoying? But that is my rule because there are other activities that are important to build your mind and body. I am not asking you to like or agree with the rule. Rulemaking is mommy's job. When I take the tablet away, I know you might be upset. When you are done being upset, we can find something else to do together."

Luisa comes up with limits that she has the power to implement. When tablet time is over, Luisa explains: "It is time to put the tablet away. That is going to happen. How it happens is up to you. You have two great choices: You can give the tablet back to me, which means you will have the chance to use it again tomorrow. If you choose not to cooperate with putting it away, I will have to take it from you, even if that feels uncomfortable, and there will be no screen time tomorrow." She tells Mateo that, since this is a really big decision, she is going to put on a timer for a full minute to give him a chance to think about his choice. (Some parents find that reducing the time to 30 seconds works better for their kids. The point is to give them some amount of time to use their thinking versus reactive brain.) This approach to setting limits enables Luisa to control the situation while not trying to control Mateo.

The Outcome

The first time Luisa enacts the new plan, Mateo runs away with the tablet with that mischievous laugh that really yanks her chain. She has to exert tremendous self-control not to start shouting at him to wipe that smile off of his face. (She knows from our discussion about her faulty mindsets that Mateo's laughter in these charged moments does not signal that he is a sociopath. He is reacting to the ambivalence and discomfort some children experience in these moments when they are being defiant in pursuit of their goal despite their awareness that they are doing something that is making you unhappy.)

Luisa extricates the tablet from Mateo's hands while he hangs onto it as if his life depends on it. This feels very uncomfortable to her, but she stays calm and nonreactive. She doesn't say a word. (This is very important—she has already been clear about the limit and what Mateo should expect. There is no need to re-explain. Using a lot of language in these moments tends to just fuel the flames.)

Luisa places the tablet on a shelf that Mateo can't reach. Mateo starts shouting that she has to give it back—he wasn't done with his game. Luisa acknowledges his upset and starts playing with his trains. She tells him she can't wait for him to join her when he's ready. He whines and cries for a while, begging for the tablet. This is interspersed with "obnoxious" comments that Luisa ignores. Without any fodder to continue the fight, Mateo eventually joins Luisa to play with the trains.

The next day, when Mateo asks to watch a video, Luisa reminds him that there are no screens because he made the decision not to give the tablet back when time was up yesterday. This sends Mateo into another meltdown. Luisa responds that she knows this is disappointing to him and that tomorrow he can make a different decision when tablet time is up. Again, she moves on, this time to make dinner. She tells Mateo she'd love a helper in the kitchen when he's ready. He doesn't join her, but he eventually calms down.

On day three—victory. When morning tablet time is up, Luisa gives Mateo his minute to decide whether he will give it to her or she needs to be a helper and take it from him. With 20 seconds remaining, he hands it over.

With this small success, Luisa starts taking the same approach with other limits she wants to set. Once Mateo experiences that tantrums don't result in a lot of attention or getting his way, they become less frequent, and he starts to make choices that lead to more desirable outcomes for him.

Mateo especially loves having the minute to make his choices. It cracks him up. He almost always wants to tell Luisa right away what his decision is, but she responds, *"Oh, wait. You still have 50 seconds. Hold on until it's time."* He jumps around excitedly, bursting at the seams to announce his decision. This little game throws a monkey wrench into the old negativity of these battles and adds a lighthearted, fun element to the decision-making process.

GIGI: TANTRUMS IN THE TOY STORE

Greg is taking two-and-a-half-year-old Gigi to the toy store to get a birthday present for her cousin. Greg is very clear that Gigi will not be getting a toy this time. She is sanguine with this limit all the way to the mall. But after just five minutes in the store, Gigi grabs an adorable stuffed unicorn off the shelf, holds it close to her chest, and proclaims, "My horsie!"

Greg, annoyed, reminds Gigi that she won't be getting a toy today and so the answer is "no." Gigi throws herself on the floor, kicking and screaming. Greg tells her she has to stop right now! The more he demands that she stop the tantrum, the more out of control Gigi becomes. Meanwhile, Greg gets increasingly worked up, mortified by this public display of disaster.

He makes threats: "You won't get any TV time today if you don't stop this tantrum." No impact. He tries bribery: "If you stop scream-ing, I will get you a toy next time." She responds: "No! I need horsie now." Worn down and desperately wanting to put an end to the embarrassing public spectacle, Greg relents and buys the unicorn, angrily exclaiming, "Fine! But this is the last toy I am buying you for the whole year!"

Greg feels horrible about the not-infrequent encounters like this with Gigi. He hates losing it with her but doesn't know how to make her accept the limits he is trying to set without bribery. And he is horrified thinking about how Gigi's behavior looks to others who witness these moments. He just wants to end the tantrums—whatever he has to do—which he has started to call "the-path-of-least-resistance parenting."

The Mindsets and Mindshifts

As we think through this and other similar scenarios that lead to Gigi having a tantrum, the first insight for Greg is that *he expects Gigi to have more self-control than she is actually capable of.* Two-year-olds are in the early stages of learning to manage their impulses. Their desires almost always prevail over what is "right." They may agree to a rule or limit in theory, but, in the moment, their desires will almost always rule the day. Once Greg sees Gigi's meltdowns through the lens of development and makes the mindshift *that she is not misbehaving on purpose; she is acting her age and needs time, practice, and support to learn to manage when she can't get what she wants,* he moves from anger and frustration to empathy.

Dissecting these encounters also leads to the realization that *trying to get Gigi to change her behavior—to not have a meltdown to begin with and then to get calm once she does—is backfiring.* Trying to talk her out of her feelings only throws her into further distress; and, offering rewards, when she does accept them, effectively puts her in charge. She is dictating the rules of engagement, which sets a pattern of her not cooperating with any rules or directions without demanding a reward. These shifts in mindset motivate Greg to focus on what he *can* do to be supportive of Gigi in these challenging moments—which means staying present and loving while also setting clear boundaries that will help her get calm and cope.

The Plan

Greg lets Gigi know exactly what to expect. "We are going to the grocery store. I know there are so many yummy things there that you may want. When we get there, you will be able to pick a box of raisins or cheese crackers as a snack. We are not going to be getting any cookies or candy."

He lets her know what the plan will be if she has a hard time coping with the limit. Greg tells Gigi that he completely understands that it is hard for her when she can't get something she wants. And, sometimes, she gets so mad that she goes into the red zone, when her whole mind and body feel out of control (she's screaming, kicking, hitting, etc.). Greg lets Gigi know that, if that happens, he will try to help her calm down with deep belly breathing or by giving her a bear hug. (See the appendix for more calming tools.) If she is not able to use one of these tools to calm down and move along, he will be a helper. If they are at the grocery store, he will place her in the shopping cart and strap her in to keep her safe. If they are elsewhere, for example, taking a walk or at the playground, he is going to bring a stroller so that he can keep her secure and help her move on safely.

The Outcome

Greg is very consistent about the limits in the grocery store, which results in Gigi adapting and accepting one of the choices he has offered, most of the time. But now when Gigi melts down, Greg doesn't try to talk her out of it. He acknowledges her feelings and lets her know that, if she needs to be upset, that's okay. It's her mind and body. If they are home, he gives her space until she is calm and ready to re-engage in a new activity.

When Gigi melts down in a public space, he calmly helps her move on. He ignores her kicking and screaming as he straps her into a stroller or carries her to the car and, instead, talks about what they will do at home or sings a silly song to show her he's not mad at her. He is just helping her to get back in control by taking her out of the triggering situation.

Greg is now clear that he can't make Gigi stop having tantrums, but he can respond to them in a way that doesn't exacerbate them. By not relying on rewards to help Gigi cope with disappointment and sticking to the limits calmly and lovingly, Gigi learns to cope with not getting what she wants—which is what ultimately leads to fewer tantrums.

(To learn more about how to deal with public meltdowns, see the guidance at the end of this chapter.)

LUCAS AND THE LOW FRUSTRATION TOLERANCE

Four-year-old Lucas has a very low tolerance for frustration. The second he faces a challenge he gives up. Often, he is triggered into the red zone and has a full-on meltdown. Recently his dad, Russell, bought him a scooter. When Lucas excitedly hops onto it, he loses his balance and falls off. He promptly tosses the scooter and shouts, "This is the stupidest scooter. I never wanted one anyway!" Russell tries to coax and cajole Lucas to keep trying. Lucas responds: "Stop talking to me right now!" Russell is becoming very anxious about what he sees as Lucas's lack of confidence and perseverance. He doesn't want Lucas to feel bad about himself, so Russell says that scooters aren't for everyone and puts it away.

This kind of reaction is rampant: Lucas quits playing tag with his group of friends when he gets tagged out early in the game. He regularly knocks down elaborate structures he has built when he can't get one block to fit the way he wants. Russell runs to the rescue, quieting Lucas with a snack on the sidelines while Russell rebuilds the tower.

The Mindsets and Mindshifts

When Russell and I first meet, he is very worried about the lack of grit he sees in Lucas. He wonders how Lucas is going to succeed in life if he keeps giving up so easily. Russell is a doer and a problem solver. He knows that Lucas's lack of ability to muscle through typical life challenges does not bode well for him. But this anxiety about Lucas's lack of confidence has resulted in Russell running to the rescue to make it all better. *Russell believes that it is Lucas's negative narrative about himself—that he is a failure—that is the cause of his giving up so easily.*

As Russell and I analyze these scenarios, Russell begins to see that, in fact, it is *Russell's efforts to fix all of Lucas's problems that is perpetuating, not putting an end to, Lucas's sense of failure.* It sends Lucas the message that Russell doesn't believe Lucas can master the challenge he is facing and needs Russell to make it all better. *What Lucas needs is support to learn to manage his frustration and feel confident to work through the struggles he encounters.*

Further, as we do the detective work to figure out what the root cause might be of Lucas's low frustration tolerance, temperament emerges as a major factor. Russell describes Lucas as living life on the extremes—he is either ecstatic or enraged. He reacts to his experiences in the world with great intensity, which means he feels overwhelmed a lot of the time. He is on a hair trigger for feeling out of control. When things don't go the way he wants or expects, he goes from zero to 60 in a split second.

With these insights, Russell sees that, by changing his response to Lucas, he has the power to help Lucas see himself as competent and resilient.

The Plan

Russell stops jumping to the rescue. When Lucas faces a challenge and starts to fall apart, Russell calmly names the problem and shows empathy: "Learning to balance on a scooter takes time. I know it's uncomfortable for you when something doesn't work right away. I understand."

He gives Lucas space to recover. He avoids trying to convince or cajole Lucas to keep working at it because this often escalates the situation. (As counterintuitive as it may seem, trying to get children to keep trying often increases their anxiety. They sense that it is important to the parent that they succeed at the task at hand, which puts more pressure on them and amplifies the shame they are already experiencing about their perceived failure.)

Russell positions himself as Lucas's problem-solving partner. He lets Lucas know that he has confidence in his ability to learn to solve the problems he encounters and that he can do hard things. He explains to Lucas that daddy will always help him think through the challenges he faces and help him come up with solutions but he won't solve his problems for him because that is Lucas's job. In this vein, Russell lets Lucas know that, when he's ready to try again, daddy is happy to be a helper. And he always asks for permission before sharing his ideas, rather than launching into his suggestions: "I have some ideas about how to help you balance on the scooter. Let me know if you'd like to hear them." (Offering unsolicited guidance, especially when your child is in a stressed state, can feel intrusive and intensify his distress. Asking for permission to provide input shows respect for your child's boundaries and makes it more likely that he will actually absorb the ideas you are sharing.)

Russell helps Lucas think through the natural outcome of his choices. Previously, Russell's anxiety about the negative consequences of Lucas's giving up so quickly would result in schooling Lucas on the negative outcome of his reactions: "You'll never learn to ride a scooter if you keep giving up." "No one is going to want to play tag or other games with you if you quit when you're not the winner." Russell now sees that these kinds of responses only increase Lucas's feelings of shame and result in a defensive posture that doesn't help him work through his feelings.

Instead, Russell helps Lucas think about the outcome of his actions. First, he matter-of-factly recounts the story of what happened: "You hopped on the scooter with so much excitement. It tipped over. That felt uncomfortable to you. That made you want the scooter to go away." (Recounting the story matter-of-factly opens kids up to taking a more objective look at their actions and their outcomes.)

Russell asks questions that get Lucas's wheels turning, such as "After you quit the scooter/game of tag, what happened?" "How did you feel?" "Is there a different way you would have liked it to have ended?" "How could you make that happen?" (Approaching a situation by seeking to understand without criticism or judgment provides an opportunity for your child to make connections between his actions and their outcomes.)

Russell provides the support Lucas needs to master the challenge. He assesses what Lucas needs and refrains from doing something Lucas can do himself. If Lucas is having trouble stabilizing the structure he is building, Russell helps Lucas think through a solution but doesn't start inserting blocks to make the building balance. When Lucas says he's ready to try the scooter again, Russell provides enough support to help Lucas feel secure enough to take the next step.

The Outcome

When Lucas says he is ready to try the scooter again, Russell asks Lucas what kind of help he would like. Lucas wants Russell to hold him and push the scooter—essentially doing the entire thing for Lucas. Russell agrees to do this for a few minutes to help Lucas have the experience of feeling safe and secure on the scooter.

Once Lucas is comfortable on the scooter, Russell tells Lucas he has some ideas for how to help Lucas learn to balance on his own and asks if he would like to hear them. Yes, he would. Russell suggests that he hold onto the handlebars while Lucas just stands on the scooter while it is stationary. Once Lucas feels comfortable in this position, they agree that the next step should be Russell's pulling Lucas on the scooter along the driveway as Russell continues to hold the handlebars. Russell then asks whether Lucas would like to push the scooter on his own, but Lucas isn't ready for that step yet. Russell refrains from doing any cheerleading or coaxing (e.g., "But you're doing so well. You can do it, bud"). The next day, Lucas announces that he wants to push the scooter on his own while Russell is still holding on. Taking this incremental approach, with Russell slowly pulling back on his support, Lucas is scootering independently and masterfully by the end of the week.

With the positive and promising outcome of this experience, Russell takes the same approach whenever Lucas is frustrated in the face of a challenge. Over time, he starts to see a significant change in Lucas: he is having far fewer meltdowns and is much more resilient overall. Not only is Lucas feeling more empowered, having adopted an "I can do it!" attitude, but the relationship between Russell and Lucas flourishes.

RAINE: "I SAID I WANT THE RED BOWL!"

Raine, age five, is fierce. She has very strong ideas about how things should be and has a hard time coping when something happens that she does not expect. She melts down upon discovering that her dad, Seth, has filled the bathtub when *she* wanted to turn on the faucet. She demands he drain the tub. When her mom, Tamara, comes to pick her up from school, instead of grandma, whom Raine was expecting, she hides under the table and insists Tamara go home. When Seth puts her cereal in the blue bowl instead of her favorite red bowl, she hurls the bowl off the table and refuses to eat.

Seth and Tamara are exhausted. They find themselves giving in to her totally irrational demands just to get some peace. They know this is not a good dynamic, but they are tired of the tantrums and just worn down.

The Mindsets and Mindshifts

When we talk about the feelings that are getting triggered for Seth and Tamara when Raine is acting "insane," what emerges is that they are angry and frustrated with her. *She is such a smart little girl—she shouldn't be acting so irrationally.* They see lots of other kids the same age who don't go nuts like this over seemingly minor issues. They expected tantrums when she was two and three, and maybe even four, but not five.

As Seth and Tamara go into more detail about what makes Raine tick, a picture emerges of a very sensitive, intense little girl whose brain never shuts off. She processes all her experiences at a very deep level, which leaves her feeling overwhelmed much of the time. To make the world feel more manageable, she comes up with very fixed ideas about how things should be. When something unexpected happens, she has a hard time coping. Her boiling point is low due to her sensitivity, so she loses it more easily. *Seeing Raine's behavior through the lens of temperament helps Seth and Tamara recalibrate their expectations; that it is not just Raine's age that impacts her ability to self-regulate but also her temperament.*

This insight also leads to a mindshift *from seeing Raine's efforts to get her way as manipulative to understanding that she is just trying to cope.* They understand, now, that Raine's irrational demands are rooted in her effort to try to control all of her experiences in the world. She is going to do whatever it takes to stay in her comfort zone (a natural, human drive). They see that what Raine needs from them is support to learn to be more flexible so she can adapt when things don't or can't happen the way she wants or expects. This means they have to get comfortable with Raine's discomfort. They need to tolerate her temporary unhappiness to be able to set the limits necessary for her to experience that she can survive when things don't go exactly the way she expects. Helping her become more flexible is what will help her be happy in the long run.

The Plan

Tamara and Seth start with empathy. They acknowledge that Raine has very strong and clear ideas about how things should be; and that it's uncomfortable for her when something unexpected happens, like when mommy shows up at school when she was thinking that grandma would be coming.

They teach her about flexibility. They tell Raine that they will always notify her in advance of any changes they are aware of but acknowledge that things sometimes happen at the last minute that they can't prepare for. There will be times when someone else has to pick her up because grandma is stuck at a doctor's appointment; mommy, the bedtime book reader, has to work late, so daddy will read the stories; or the grocery store will be out of the brand of chicken nuggets Raine likes so she has to choose another kind. All of these experiences are part of life because nobody can control everything. They explain that it is their job to help her learn to be flexible so she can adapt when she can't have what she wants or expects.

They give her a sense of control when she has to cope with a limit. They always give her two great choices, such as whether she wants to be pushed on the swing or climb on the monkey bars before it's time to leave the playground. (What is *not* a choice is whether to leave the playground when it's time to go. Remember the difference between directions and choices!)

The Outcome

Seth and Tamara follow through with this approach, which requires a heavy dose of self-control. When Tamara shows up at school, instead of grandma, and Raine starts screaming for her to go away, Tamara calmly acknowledges Raine's upset: she understands that it is a surprise for Raine to see mom and she needs to adjust to that idea. Tamara then tells Raine that it is time to get in the car, but how she gets in is up to her. Her two great choices are to walk, holding mom's hand, or mom will be a helper and carry her. When Raine resists, Tamara scoops her up and buckles her into her car seat. Once settled in, Tamara asks Raine which song she wants to listen to. Raine keeps screaming that she wants grandma. Tamara puts on a song and starts to sing along. By the time they get home, Raine is calm. Tamara comments that Raine did a great job of coping with this unexpected event. (Even when a child protests, it is important to focus on the fact that she survived the upset. That is the key message we want kids to get: that while an experience might be uncomfortable, they can handle it. That's what builds resilience and flexibility.)

When Raine's favorite red cereal bowl is dirty, they acknowledge her disappointment and let her know she can choose another bowl. (I know. You're thinking what's the big deal about just washing the red bowl to avoid yet another meltdown. That would indeed be easier in the short run, but this is a long-term issue: to help Raine learn to accept and see that she can survive not getting exactly what she thinks she needs and can't live without.) Tamara puts out several bowls and lets Raine know she should tell them when she is ready to make her decision. Then, they move on. They don't respond to her continued protestations or whining, but they stay present, talking to each other about things Raine is interested in, like dinosaurs, and telling jokes that she loves, to show her that they aren't going to engage in a protracted battle but are eager to stay connected with her. When Raine won't budge and refuses to eat, Seth and Tamara don't get reactive; they don't go into the gray zone by trying to get her to agree with their limit. When they stay the course and Raine sees they aren't going to resurrect the red bowl, she eventually asks for cereal in a coffee mug! (Even kids don't want to eat crow.) Seth comments, "You were so flexible! Your brain was telling you that you were going to get the red bowl, but, when it wasn't available, you were able to be flexible and choose another option!

As Seth and Tamara continue on this path of acknowledging and accepting Raine's feelings and giving her choices within acceptable limits, there is a major reduction in power struggles. Raine becomes better able to tolerate the unexpected and be more flexible overall—a gift that keeps on giving.

KEY STEPS FOR RESPONDING EFFECTIVELY TO TANTRUMS

Practice prevention. Use what you know from past experiences with your child to anticipate what kinds of situations may be challenging for her. For example, if you know that leaving Grandpa's house is cause for a full-blown meltdown, before you leave, acknowledge that you know it is tough to say goodbye to Grandpa, and help your child make a plan for coping when it's time to go. You might have her choose a book she can bring with her to Grandpa's. Before it's time to leave, she and Grandpa can read halfway through the book together. Then, when she gets home, she can video chat with Grandpa and finish reading the book remotely. Letting your child know the connection will continue and giving her something positive to focus on when she has to end an activity she enjoys can reduce the distress of the transition. But if the meltdown happens . . .

Do a parent self-check. You are already well-aware from reading anything on parenting that has come out in the past 10 years, and from your own experiences in the trenches with your kids, that managing your own emotions is the foundation of responding calmly and effectively in challenging moments with your children. But for most parents, this is easier said than done. This is where the "mommy/daddy moment" strategy comes in (which was introduced in chapter 2, on cooperation). It can reduce reactivity when it's not a life-threatening situation (your child isn't running into the street). It gives you a minute to think through what is in front of you and what your child needs in that moment, to give yourself time to consider your response and to think about what you do and don't control in this situation, rather than reacting in the heat of the moment and getting bogged down in the gray zone trying to coax your child out of his upset.

You start by putting words to what's going on: "You are really upset about having to say goodbye to grandpa." Acknowledging your child's experience without judgment or anger can be very calming to him. Mirroring his emotional experience is soothing to his nervous system.[12]

Then, you announce that you are going to take a mommy/daddy moment to figure out how you can help him cope. You might tap your head as you say aloud, "Hmm, Charlie is having a hard time leaving grandpa. That makes total sense—he loves grandpa, so why would he want to leave? But it's time to go home for dinner, so how can I help him move on? I can't *make* him get into the car. It's his body—only he can decide that. But I can give him two great choices: either he can choose to walk to the car on his own or I can be a helper and carry him there." It's often very amusing to kids to see and hear their parents' thought process. Sometimes, this results in the child snapping out of it and cooperating. But even if it doesn't, you have had the chance to make a more mindful decision; and one, most importantly, whose outcome you control. To boot, it provides a powerful model of problem solving and self-control.

Examine your mindset. In this mommy/daddy moment, think about what narrative is taking place in your head regarding the situation. There might be some faulty, unhelpful notions percolating, as the examples illustrate in the stories in this chapter. Are you trying to control your child? Do you think your child is purposefully trying to drive you mad or he is just struggling to cope with a challenging situation? Think about whether there is a mindshift that needs to take place so that these faulty mindsets don't get in the way of responding calmly and effectively.

Empathize with your child. In your mommy/daddy moment, remind yourself that the toddler brain has very little ability to control strong emotions and that your child is not trying to make your life harder. She is just having a hard time coping. She needs your understanding and support and to feel a positive connection to you, even as she is melting down.

Be sure to acknowledge and accept, not judge, your child's feelings. Remember, feelings are never the problem; it's what kids (and we adults!) do with their feelings that can be productive or problematic. The more you help your child identify and accept her feelings ("It's really hard for you when you're not the winner of the game" or "You hate to leave the park when your friends are still playing"), the better able she will be to manage them in healthy ways.

Avoid a big reaction to provocative behavior. If your child lays into you and hurls vitriol ("You are the meanest, stupidest mommy. I hate you!"), *don't* react to her words but *do* validate the underlying feeling: "I know you are mad that I am taking you home. It's okay to be angry. I am not asking or expecting you to like that we have to leave. But we still need to go." You can't stop your child from saying nasty things to you when she's triggered, but you can ignore the provocation and address the root cause. Any big reaction reinforces the unwanted behavior.

In fact, it can be very effective to use a little reverse psychology, especially with the really feisty kids who are more prone to defiance. When they melt down in the face of a limit you have set, you acknowledge that you see they are having a hard time with your decision and that it's okay for them to be upset for however long it takes until they can calm down. Time after time, I have witnessed this parental response result in children doing a full reversal. They proclaim, in one way or another, "I don't need any more time!" To assert their independence, they snap out of it.

Limit language when enforcing a limit. Too much talking can be overwhelming to children when they are in the red zone and are so distressed that they have lost control of their minds and bodies. Their brains are flooded with emotion, so there is no bandwidth for processing any information or ideas you want to communicate. It's best to make a calming statement in a low, calm voice: "Those are big feelings. I am here. I'll help you get through this. You are not alone."

Stay connected with your child. Even as your child is melting down and perhaps pushing you away with her words or actions, show her that you love her so much that you are not going to participate in this negative interaction. You are still very much there for her and are staying connected.

Let's say your child is running in the parking lot and won't stop when you say freeze. You have to pick her up and place her in her car seat as she is thrashing and screaming. The only thing you say is "I will always keep you safe." No lecturing or reprimanding. That only fuels the flames and falls on deaf ears because your child's brain is closed in the red zone. She is not losing it on purpose. She needs you to be her rock as she is unraveling.

Once she's strapped safely into the car seat, you move on. There is no need to try to teach a lesson through words. You have shown with your actions that you are always going to keep her safe when she is doing something dangerous. Instead, try asking her a silly question or playing dumb about something. "I can't remember; is the green train Percy or Thomas?" Taking this approach often has the desired effect of engaging your child in something productive—like supplying the answer to your question—and throwing a monkey wrench into her downward spiral. If this doesn't work and she keeps up the protests, just keep moving along: "No problem; we can always talk about the trains later." The key is to show you are calm, loving, and in control—exactly what your child needs in these moments.

Engage in joint problem solving (with children over two and a half). Problem solving can happen only once your child is calm. His brain cannot take in any information when he is in the red zone. When the storm has subsided, comment on what a great job he did calming himself down (no matter how long it took). You want to emphasize that he can survive these upsets. Then, recount the incident in a very matter-of-fact way, without any judgment or criticism. "You love visiting Grandpa. You had so much fun building that giant city for the dinosaurs. So, when it was time to leave, you felt really sad and mad at me for making you go. Sometimes, you don't like the rules I make. I understand." Then, brainstorm ways to cope next time he has to leave a situation he is really enjoying. That's when you might introduce the book idea described above. Some families establish a special "see-you-next-time" kiss or snap a photo to send to Grandpa's phone on the way home as a way to stay connected. The more your child feels involved in coming up with the solution, the more likely it is that he will follow through on it in the moment.

Expect things to get worse before they get better. When you make a change in your strategy for setting limits and dealing with meltdowns, children initially protest harder or have a bigger tantrum.

Their reactions become fiercer due to the natural discomfort they feel when you aren't doing the dance they are used to. They test you to see whether this new plan will hold. But, if you stay the course, calmly and lovingly, your child will eventually adapt to the new program.

When Your Child Loses It in Public

Most parents of young children live in terror of their little one losing it in public. It's hard to avoid feeling judged and ashamed of out-of-control behavior, as if it were evidence of your incompetence as a parent. This naturally puts most moms and dads in an emotionally charged place, feeling embarrassed and often angry at their child for putting them in this deeply uncomfortable and stressful situation.

The mindshift to make is that *your child is not losing it nor misbehaving on purpose.* Whether she breaks down because of overstimulation, a common trigger for tantrums in public places, or you have set a limit she doesn't like, she has lost control and is unable to cope on her own. Taking any kind of revved-up or harsh approach or trying to talk her out of her upset is likely to exacerbate the situation.

Here are some ways to handle these moments that can help you feel more effective and less mortified.

Stay calm. If you are anxious and upset, your child is more likely to be anxious and upset. If you are calm and composed, she is likely to pull herself together more quickly. While your emotional reaction is completely understandable, it is not strategic to have a big reaction. When she is falling apart, she needs you to be her rock. It's best to take a few deep breaths and remind yourself that, if you decompensate too, you will likely make the situation more stressful and challenging for both of you.

Validate your child's feelings. "I know you are unhappy that they don't have apple juice at this restaurant. Your brain was thinking that you would be having it with your lunch. I understand your disappointment." Validating feelings is not the same as validating behavior. Remember, feelings aren't the problem; it is what kids do with their feelings that can be problematic (also true for parents). That's why one of your most important jobs is to help your child learn to manage these strong, difficult emotions in acceptable ways. But that takes time and practice. And it starts with validation—the first step in helping children identify and then manage their feelings.

Provide choices, when possible, that you can implement. In the case above, this might mean offering your child a choice of two other beverages. Even when you offer what seems like great alternatives, your child may flat-out reject them and intensify the tantrum to show you just how lame he thinks these other options are. In that case, you might calmly respond: "I know, nothing feels right. Let's go take a break. Do you want to walk holding my hand, or do you want me to be a helper and put you in the stroller?" If your child can't pull himself together, place him in the stroller (or cart or car seat, depending on the situation you're in) with as much calm as you can muster. Ignore all his efforts to get you to react. Start talking about anything else but the incident at hand, as that is only likely to inflame your child further. For example, if you are in the grocery store, you might talk about what you see in the different aisles as you make your exit. This lets your child know that you can handle his upset and will always stay present and connected, even when he is spiraling out of control.

Leaving the restaurant, grocery store, or whatever public venue you are in may feel like giving in, but consider the alternative: if you can't actually control your child and he is being destructive or disruptive to others and/or you are losing control yourself (given that you are, in fact, only human), then staying in place is likely to be much more detrimental to you and your child than moving on. What's most important is that you are able to maintain control and remain as calm as possible. This teaches your child that you will always be his "safe base" no matter the situation.

Don't let the onlookers get to you. Ideally, just tune them out. Most of them are likely feeling your pain, having been there themselves, and aren't judging. And even for those voyeurs feeling some guilty pleasure that they are not in the hot seat, or those who think they know better, ignoring is still a good strategy. Your energy is better spent staying focused on coming up with a productive response to helping your child cope.

Or kill them with kindness. If a bystander makes some really helpful comment (sarcastic font), avoid being reactive. You have nothing to be defensive about. Instead, try something like this: "It is so nice that you want to help. I really appreciate it. But I'm all good. Learning that he can't get everything he wants is a hard lesson for a little guy, right?" This is a nice way to send some important messages: "I am in control, and I am being a really good parent by setting appropriate limits and helping my child learn to cope with life's disappointments." This can be a particularly good strategy when it is your parent, in-law, close friend, or family member who is trying to help.

Most importantly, try not to allow your worry about bystanders' opinions and judgments drive your behavior in these situations. Many parents report that they end up giving in to their child's demands to avoid embarrassment, even though they don't think that's best for their child. You have nothing to be embarrassed about— all toddlers have tantrums. And when you give in, your child is cleverly putting two and two together: "Mommy or daddy will pretty much give me anything to get me to quiet down when we're outside the house!"

When you respond calmly and with empathy and set clear limits that you can enforce, you send both your child and the onlookers the message that you're all good, calm and in control.

Next, we turn to situations when your child loses control to the point that she is being physically aggressive or destructive.

4

PHYSICAL AGGRESSION

When Alex, age five, places a cup down on the glass coffee table, his mom, Charlotte, tells him that he needs to be gentle. He responds, "It's not fragile! *Don't ever say that to me again! Do you understand? Do you understand?*," as he kicks her. This reaction is not atypical; Alex explodes like this on a regular basis when his parents, Charlotte and Kevin, need to correct him or set a limit, or even when they make seemingly benign suggestions, such as how to hold the scissors correctly. When these outbursts occur, Alex frequently becomes verbally and physically aggressive. The more his parents try to reason with him—telling him that it's no big deal and that he's overreacting—the more distressed he becomes.

This behavior extends outside the home. A typical scenario took place recently at Alex's kiddie soccer program. He kicked the ball toward the goal, but another child, Ellie, kicked it away. Alex started shouting that Ellie cheated and then pushed her as he stormed off the field. This is Alex's typical reaction whenever he does not immediately succeed at something and especially when he loses in a competitive situation. He lashes out physically and then quits.

Charlotte and Kevin are very worried about Alex's lack of self-control and their inability to help him get calm and better cope with what they see as small, expectable challenges.

Few things are more vexing to a parent than when their child is physically aggressive by hitting, kicking, pushing, biting, or pinching. Many parents I work with worry that this kind of behavior signals a lack of empathy. One dad recently voiced what many parents find perplexing: "How could we—such loving, peaceful people—have created a child who can be so hurtful?"

At the same time, parents fear the consequences for their child (Will she be seen as a bully? Will other children not want to play with him? Will she get kicked out of preschool?) and for themselves (Will I be alienated from the other parents who judge me because of my child's behavior?).

These are all very natural concerns, which understandably trigger intense emotions that can lead to harsh and punitive parental responses that often backfire, escalating the aggressive behavior. These reactions are rooted in two very powerful mindsets: *my child is misbehaving on purpose* and *my child harbors malicious intent when she is hurtful*.

I find that most parents expect that, by age three, their child should be able to control her impulses, that it is in their child's power to stop herself from acting out physically in moments of distress. They don't see other children the same age being aggressive, so they assume that their child is making a conscious choice to be harmful. Common responses in these moments include "What is wrong with you? Why would you want to hurt Mommy? You are making me so sad." "No one will ever want to play with you if you hurt them."

THERE ARE A NUMBER OF IMPORTANT FACTORS THAT LEAD TO AGGRESSIVE BEHAVIOR THAT ARE VERY IMPORTANT TO KEEP IN MIND

Development. The "upstairs brain" (the prefrontal cortex), which enables us to exert control over our impulses and to be able to think about our feelings and plan an effective response, is just starting to develop around age three; but that does not mean children are anywhere near able to *consistently* manage their impulses. For example, while a three-year-old can tell you that, indeed, it would be best to use his words to ask a classmate to return a toy she has grabbed out of his hand, he may still whack that peer in a moment of frustration and anger. Researchers who study self-regulation explain that three-year-olds know logically that it is better to wait, but just knowing this isn't enough.[13] There is a growing body of research that shows that the prefrontal cortex is not fully developed until the third decade of life.[14] Learning to manage our minds and bodies is a decades-long process.

Temperament. Temperament is an important variable that impacts whether a child is more or less likely to be physically aggressive. Children who are highly sensitive—big reactors by nature—tend to have lower thresholds for stress. They are triggered into a state of dysregulation more quickly than other children and are thus likely to act more impulsively. In the moment, when they are on system overload, their bodies react faster than their brains. (Resources on the neurobiology of stress in children can be found in the appendix.)

Another aspect of temperament that often goes undetected is rooted in a child's *sensory processing functioning*—the way the nervous system receives information from the senses and turns it into behavioral responses.[15] For example, a child walks into preschool and is able to navigate around the kids scattered across the classroom who are engaged in different activities so as not to bump into them, walk over them, or accidentally destroy whatever it is they may be working on (a block tower or a train track). She automatically "reads the room" and responds appropriately. On the other hand, a child whose system is not processing this visual–spatial information accurately and who doesn't have a firm grasp of where her body is in space may end up looking like a bull in a china shop and inadvertently hurt peers or objects in the process.

Children whose sensory processing systems are not working effectively often feel bombarded with sensations they can't manage effectively. They are overresponsive to sensory input; for example, Marcello, age two and a half, who throws huge fits every morning if his favorite comfy sweatpants aren't available. He won't go near a pair of buttoned or zippered pants, not because he is being irrational or spoiled, but because his sensory processing system is not registering his tactile experiences accurately, in this case making the closures on clothing unbearable. Sensations that other children are not bothered by are very uncomfortable for him. Or Samantha, age three, who is oversensitive to a range of sensory experiences—lights are too bright, sounds are too blaring, or people are too close. When she is feeling overwhelmed, she bites to protect herself—a reflexive reaction that also happens to be a very effective strategy for keeping others at bay.

Children whose sensory systems are overresponsive in these and other ways are triggered to feel uncomfortable and overwhelmed by the world more easily. They are bombarded by sensations they cannot effectively manage. This means they melt down more frequently, intensely, and often aggressively.

On the other hand, there are children whose sensory processing systems are underresponsive to their sensory experiences in the world. They crave more intense input to feel comfortable; for example, Will, age four, whose teachers report that he can't keep his hands to himself. He is constantly getting into trouble at school for squeezing other kids' arms, putting his hands on everything in his path, leaning his body against his peers at circle time, and constantly knocking objects off the tables and shelves. The other kids are now starting to avoid playing with him.

At home, Will is also very physical in ways that are "annoying" and confusing to his parents, Tamisa and Brent. He will press his head hard against his mom's head and won't stop when she asks him to. He body slams his siblings on a regular basis. Consequences nor punishments result in reducing these behaviors.

Will is underresponsive to tactile sensations. His body craves intense levels of stimulation. He is driven to crash into or push things with great force, including people. He is the kid who accidentally knocks peers down when giving a big bear hug, without any intention of hurting them. But you can see how this need to feed his sensory system in this way results in behaviors that get labeled and are seen as purposefully "aggressive." You can also see how the sensory processing system is an important piece of the puzzle in understanding the "why" of children's behavior. (To learn more about the impact of sensory processing on children's behavior, see the resources in the appendix.)

Context: Your child's experiences in the world. Any major change, especially one that is particularly difficult or painful—such as a separation or loss or witnessing a traumatic event—can lead to acting out in aggressive ways. Recently, I met with a family whose four-year-old had seen a tree fall on their neighbor's car during a major storm. She became extremely fearful of going outside. She also started to hit and bite—new behaviors for her. Young children's brains are still in the early stages of development. The "downstairs brain," which puts us into flight, fight, or freeze mode when experiencing stress, is much more likely to drive children's behavior than the upstairs brain, which enables us to think about our feelings and experiences and manage how to best deal with those emotions. When children have experienced a highly stressful event, their psychic energy is diverted to cope with the big, confusing feelings that have gotten triggered and they are less able to calm themselves and self-regulate.

THE CRITICAL MINDSHIFTS

No child, including yours, *wants* to be hurtful. Whatever the root cause of your child's aggressive actions, she is on system overload and does not have the skills yet to cope in these moments when she is triggered into the red zone. In fact, parents report over and over that, once their children have calmed after the storm, they feel sad and confused. They don't like feeling so out of control and hurting others. They often voice frustration at their inability to calm themselves down: "It's like a monster takes over and I can't stop him." "My brain just goes crazy." And this from an incredibly self-aware five-year-old: "Mom, the other day when I said those really mean things and threw my truck at you, I was just really mad and I went nuts."

Many children also become very contrite and overcome with worry about the break in their connection with their parents following an aggressive outburst. They can't stop saying sorry and become very clingy, asking, "Are you okay, Mommy?" "Did I make you angry?" "Don't be sad, Daddy."

What children need in these moments is for you to be their rock by staying emotionally calm and connected and not taking their actions personally. That means you are not harsh or punitive, as revved-up reactions only escalate children's distress. I realize this is no small feat; guidance on this follows. But it does become easier to manage your own emotions in these tense situations when you are coming from a place of understanding and empathy versus anger.

While you can't control your child—you can't make him not hit, bite, or throw objects—you can control the situation. When your child becomes aggressive, you naturally want to make him stop, ASAP. The typical first step is to demand that your child stop hitting/biting/pushing, but this strategy rarely works because, when children are in the red zone, they are not in control of their minds or their bodies. They are not in a rational state of mind, so trying to use logic and reasoning is not only ineffective but can cause further escalation. (Think about those times when you are triggered into the red zone and your partner/spouse starts offering up suggestions for a resolution. Does this help or send you further into the stratosphere?)

Sometimes, calming methods work—giving your child a bear hug or having her take deep belly breaths. But, more often than not, parents report that the more they try to calm their child when she is in the red zone, the more agitated she becomes, leaving parents feeling completely out of control. This scenario is frightening and very destabilizing for both children and parents and makes it less likely that you will be able to gain control over an unsafe situation.

My work with Charlotte and Kevin on how to manage in these moments when Alex has lost control of his mind and body provides a road map for how to respond when your child is being physically aggressive.

ALEX: THE HIGHLY SENSITIVE, BIG REACTOR

Recall Alex who melts down and becomes physically aggressive when he is corrected, a limit is set, or he perceives he is imperfect.

The Mindsets and Mindshifts

Taking a step back, one powerful trigger that we identify as the source of Alex's aggressive behavior is the sense of vulnerability and shame he feels in any situation in which he perceives he has failed, be it not getting a goal in soccer or not holding the scissors correctly. He processes simple suggestions as criticism. He is a highly sensitive child who takes things very personally. He filters his experiences through a mindset that he expects he is going to be hurt, slighted, or made to feel less than.

This insight shifts Charlotte and Kevin's mindset, from believing that Alex should be able to control his impulses and that he is being aggressive intentionally, to seeing that he does not yet have the skills to manage his strong feelings. With this new perspective, Charlotte and Kevin also begin to see how the tactics they are using to help Alex cope with losing and to feel less easily slighted are backfiring. Cheerleading ("You're great at soccer—you make lots of goals!") and trying to reason with him ("Everybody loses") aren't working because, while these responses are logical from an adult perspective, they do not reflect Alex's experience. They fall on deaf ears because Alex is not yet open to new ideas about how to interpret and handle these complex situations. Like many parents who find themselves in these situations, Charlotte and Kevin are jumping to the rescue to try to make it all better. But minimizing or ignoring feelings doesn't make them go away; it just sends the message to your child that you are uncomfortable with his feelings. This results in lost opportunities to help your child understand and manage his emotions. (Remember, feelings are not right or wrong, good or bad. They just are. The goal is to help kids learn to manage the full range of emotions they experience.)

Charlotte and Kevin also recognize that these tactics are designed to get Alex to change his behavior, which they now know is not within their power. This insight enables them to shift their focus from trying to control Alex to responding in a way that helps him feel understood so he is ultimately more open to looking at his feelings and reconsidering his perspective.

The Plan

Charlotte and Kevin empathize with and validate Alex's emotional experience. In a quiet moment, not in the heat of the storm, they tell Alex that they see that losing is very tough for him; that he likes to feel in control and losing makes him feel out of control and uncomfortable. They also understand that, when they make a suggestion about a different way to do something, he hears it as criticism or a put-down, which feels bad inside, so bad that sometimes it makes him lose control of his mind and his body. They communicate with a tone of empathy and understanding, without any judgment, sending the message that "We see you, we get you, we accept you." They let him know that strong feelings are part of being human and that they will always be there to listen to and help him understand his emotions.

They position themselves as Alex's helper. They acknowledge that meltdowns will happen. Everyone experiences times when they are so upset that they lose control of their minds and bodies. They label this the "red zone" to provide a quick and nonjudgmental way to describe Alex's experience without having to use a lot of language. ("Oh buddy, looks like it's a "red-zone" moment. We are here to help you through the storm.")

They communicate that they know Alex doesn't mean to hurt others. They understand that, when he is in the "red zone," he has lost control and doesn't mean what he says or does. His brain is closed and is not thinking clearly. At the same time, they explain that one of their most important jobs is to make sure he doesn't behave in an unsafe way. They very intentionally refer to his harmful actions as "unsafe," instead of "aggressive," "violent," or "hurtful"—language that can be very triggering to children. Further, during the early years, a child's sense of self is being solidified and is deeply affected by the messages he gets from those around him. If a child is repeatedly told that there is something wrong with him, that he is a mean and harmful person, he internalizes these messages. They become part of his personal narrative, which he then acts on: the old self-fulfilling prophecy at work.

Charlotte and Kevin also refrain from responding to Alex's hitting/biting/pinching with hurt, anger, or sadness. (Your child doesn't mean to be harmful. When you respond as if he does, it is confusing and overwhelming. It is a big burden and can be scary for a child to feel he has the power to hurt you. This worry only escalates his distress, making it harder for him to get to a place where he can reflect on these incidents and ultimately gain more control over his actions.)

Along these lines, they also refrain from asking Alex *why* he was hurtful. Children are acting on impulse and are not being aggressive on purpose. When you ask them to explain the reasoning behind their actions, it conveys that you believe they are acting with premeditation. This adds to the shame they already feel for having lost it and hurt another person, especially when that person is you, whom they love and depend on most. Young children aren't conscious of the motivation for their actions, so they make things up to satisfy us. This can lead you down a useless rabbit hole. For example, Mariel tells her mom she pushed her friend because he said something mean to her. In fact, the teacher reports that the precipitant was that this boy had decided to play with another group of kids on the playground so Mariel was left to play by herself. While Mariel isn't literally telling the truth, she is not telling a premeditated lie. Young children are just in the beginning stages of the lifelong process of learning to make sense of and manage their complex feelings and produce a prosocial response.Mariel is acting on her hurt feelings—exactly what we expect in the early years. She is not a budding sociopath, a fear many parents have when their children tell untruths.

They let Alex know that they are not going to let him do something harmful because it is not good for *him*. Charlotte and Kevin make the focus keeping *Alex* safe, not that they are protecting other people from him, including themselves. This may be counterintuitive and antithetical to what you have heard—that the focus should be on the victim and how your child has harmed the other person. In theory, this makes sense. But I find that, in practice, the more we focus on the victim, the more shame the child who has been the aggressor experiences. This shuts him down, which makes it less likely he will learn from the experience—the ultimate goal. It's important for your child to get the message that you are concerned for *him*, that being physically aggressive is not good for him, not just that it's hurtful to others. Once he is calm, you can talk about the incident and help him begin to understand how his behavior impacts both himself and others.

They work together with Alex to create a list of calming tools. They include deep belly breaths, a bear hug from Mom or Dad, chewing on a safe object (instead of biting), throwing weighted balls, punching a weighted bag, and burrowing beneath couch cushions—an experience that can be very soothing to kids. They make a poster with photos of Alex using these tools, which he loves. They explain that, when he is getting agitated, they will help him choose one of these strategies to help his mind and body get back to a calm state. (See a more comprehensive list of calming strategies in the appendix.)

They create a cooldown space. They design a "cozy corner" in the family room that includes a kiddie tent. They let Alex choose calming items for the space—cozy pillows, books, and stuffed animals. They include going to the cooldown space as one of his tools.

They come up with a code word that they will use to signal to Alex that they see he is losing control. This gives him a chance to try to avoid the full-on, "red zone" meltdown. Alex chooses "platypus." When they use the code word, they also remind him of the calming tools he identified and direct him to the poster to see whether he can choose a tool. This is a loving way to show him that they are on his side and are his partners in helping him learn to control his body. When your child is able to use a calming tool, be sure to comment on the benefit to him by pointing out the positive outcome that results, for example, that he is able to stay at the playground longer or that you can continue building your tower together because he was able to get calm after an upset.

They establish a "safe space." Charlotte and Kevin anticipate and want to be prepared for times when none of their efforts to help Alex calm down work, such as when he won't stay in the calm-down corner and keeps chasing after them, hitting, kicking, pinching, or scratching them. They need a plan that includes their ability to stop the emotionally and often physically destructive back-and-forth that ensues when Alex is in the "red zone."

They decide to make his bedroom his safe space. Like the calm-down corner, it is a loving, cozy place. The difference is that Charlotte and Kevin can put up a boundary to prevent him from exiting before his mind and body are calm. (A child's bedroom can serve as the safe space since it is not being used as punishment but as a loving, soothing space. Some parents will choose a room that is easier to child-proof, like a spare bedroom, especially if the child shares a bedroom with a sibling. The safe space can be any room that you can make safe and secure.)

Before describing how Charlotte and Kevin designed and implemented the safe space, I am going to digress here, as this is the point in developing a plan with families that often stirs up big reactions for parents. The idea that they would leave their child in a room, especially during a time when he is in distress, feels so mean, rejecting, and harmful. Further, most parents think of this as a time-out, which they have read or heard is destructive. Indeed, there is broad agreement that the use of time-out as punishment for misbehavior is both developmentally inappropriate and ineffective. Driven by their downstairs brain, we know that children are not misbehaving on purpose, so they don't learn anything from time-outs. Further, punitive approaches tend to increase challenging behaviors. They exacerbate the distress children are already experiencing in these moments. They need our empathy and support, not anger and rejection.

The antidote to time-out has become time-in, which entails staying with your child throughout the meltdown. You act as a "coregulator," providing the support your child needs to soothe herself until a time when she is able to self-regulate. This is no doubt a great approach—to be present with your child to soothe her when she is in high-stress mode and unraveling; but only if it is, in fact, calming to your child for you to be present.

The fact is that there are times when children are so out of control that they cannot accept comfort—a scenario I have observed on countless home visits. As one parent put it, "Mariel goes to a category five in a heartbeat. There is no calming her once she is triggered. The more we try to calm her, or even if we just sit there with her so she can see she's not alone, the more out of control she gets. We are burned out and finding ourselves angry at her all the time. It is just awful." In these situations, time-in does not help to soothe the child's stress response. Being in the room with her is a stimulant and dysregulating, not calming to her nervous system. Trying to get you to give in on the limit you set that led to the breakdown keeps her revved up and on high arousal, or your efforts to help her solve a problem only cause her further distress.

A family recently sent me a video in which the mom was trying to satisfy her son's demands to arrange his blankets just so. He was hysterical and thrashing about. He would not accept her comfort and kept batting her away and then running around the room aimlessly. Desperately trying to calm him and solve the problem, this mom kept asking what he wanted, but his brain was not functioning rationally so he couldn't respond effectively. Her repeated attempts to try to get him to tell her how he wanted the blankets arranged only increaseed his agitation. Even when she stopped trying to fix the problem and just remained in the room to try to be a calming presence, her son kept clawing at her, climbing on top of her, increasing his dysregulation as she was also starting to lose control. She didn't know how to make him stop his body to keep him from hurting her. In situations like these, time-in does not help to soothe the child's stress response. Being in the room with him is a stimulant and is dysregulating, not calming to his nervous system.

Scenarios like this are concerning and scary to parents, who feel that they cannot control situations that they know are emotionally and physically destructive to everyone involved. They feel like they cannot fulfill their most foundational parental responsibility: to keep their child safe and secure. I needed to find a way to help these families establish a system that would enable them to remain loving, calm, and in control as their children are spiraling out of control.

That's where the safe space comes in. When emotions (and cortisol levels in the brain[16]) are sky-high, a break for both you and your child can be a healthier approach than the tense, often aggressive back-and-forth exchange (physical and emotional) inherent in the "red-zone" moments when you are trying to physically restrain your child and losing control yourself. That is the toxic "gray zone," or no-man's land in which there is no clear limit or boundary to guide your child's behavior. This results in an increase in dysregulation and is an obstacle to getting calm. As hard as you may work on controlling your emotions, you are only human. Taking a break from interaction in these moments can be loving and helpful, not harmful. Knowing you have a strategy that can keep your child safe is what enables you to stay calm and loving, exactly what your child needs most in these moments. It creates the mental, as well as physical, space you and your child need to prevent further escalation and to help you come back together to solve the problem when you are both calm.

The key is to implement the break in a loving and supportive, not harsh and punitive, way. Here's how Charlotte and Kevin approached the safe space.

They create a boundary to prevent Alex from being able to exit on his own. As uncomfortable as this initially feels to Charlotte and Kevin, they clearly see that Alex's ability to exit the cozy corner they had created in the family room results in their losing control over the situation, which fuels the frenzy. They now see that establishing a space with a boundary is loving, not harmful. It prevents a dynamic that is way more destructive than having Alex spend time in a cozy space with a range of toys and tools to help him calm. They decide his safe space will be his bedroom.

They choose to use a gadget that keeps the door wedged open a few inches but not wide enough for a child to squeeze out. This way they don't have to close or lock the door. They preview it with Alex so he sees exactly how it works and knows what to expect. They tell him, "This is our friend 'Mr. Door Helper.' He keeps you secure in your safe space until your body is calm." (Note that not all gadgets work for every home. You might need to use a doorknob safety cover to prevent your child from being able to open the door on her own. You can also use a gate if your child is not able to climb over it or push it down. These tools prevent children from repeatedly leaving their rooms, averting the stress for both you and your child that results when you have to get physical as you try to get him back into his room. It is much more loving to provide a safe boundary than to engage in a very unpleasant tug-of-war with your child as he pulls on the knob to open the door and you are on the outside trying to keep it closed. I have come to see that this is a much more aggressive, unhealthy parent–child interaction than securing a door safely.)

They child-proof the space. They make sure there are no dangerous objects that Alex can gain access to. They remove anything he can climb on, such as stools or chairs.

They engage Alex in designing the space. They let him choose from a range of acceptable items that can be included, such as stuffed animals, squishy balls, cozy pillows, and books. They move the kiddie tent to his room because Alex likes the snuggly and comforting feeling it provides, especially when he is unraveling. (Creating a warm, friendly space communicates to your child that it is not for punishment— it is a loving space. Still, don't expect your child to thank you for putting him in his safe space. Remember, just because a child doesn't like a limit doesn't mean it's not good for him. And you are not asking for his agreement with the plan. It is a mommy/daddy responsibility to keep him safe.)

They stay as calm as possible when moving Alex to the safe space. When Alex is not able or willing to go to the safe space on his own, they need to carry him there. Even as they hold him at arm's length to avoid his kicking, hitting, or biting, they try to stay calm and keep language to a minimum. (Remember, kids can't process more input when they are in the "red zone." Their brains are flooded with emotion, and they can't think rationally.) They whisper a calming statement: "I know that it's hard right now. This will pass."

In situations when they don't feel they can get Alex into the safe space, Charlotte and Kevin go to their own safe space. Charlotte finds there are times when Alex is thrashing to the point where she does not feel she can safely move him to his bedroom. In these situations, she takes her own break. Charlotte calmly tells Alex, "I am going to my bedroom. I know you don't mean to hurt me, and I am going to prevent that from happening. When you are back in control of your body, I will come out, and we can work on solving the problem. I can't wait until we can get back to playing." (This strategy often results in the child's accepting one of his calming tools in order to keep the parent with him.)

They choose a time limit that they find is best suited for Alex. Charlotte and Kevin let him know they will return in five minutes to check on him. They use a visual timer so he knows exactly what to expect. (Some parents choose to end the break when their child is calm. Either way, once your child is back in control or is willing to accept being comforted, you can help him move on.)

They have appropriate expectations for what the break will accomplish. Charlotte and Kevin now know that Alex does not yet have the ability to reflect on his actions and behavior without their help, and that the goal of taking a break is not self-reflection. ("Gee, I wonder why I let my emotions get the best of me—I really shouldn't have scratched and kicked Daddy when he turned the TV off" is beyond toddlers and even preschoolers, not to mention many adults!) The goal is to provide a quiet place where Alex can move from a state of high agitation and upset to a sense of calm. The break offers the space for everyone to regroup. They see that no learning takes place when Alex is in a highly agitated state.

They reflect on the encounter once Alex is calm and his brain is open. They recount the incident matter-of-factly, without judgment or shaming. They want to head off any defensiveness and help Alex feel safe to look at his feelings and begin to make connections between his actions and their outcomes—the critical first step to ultimately being able to take responsibility for his behavior and make positive changes. They also want to send him the important message that they have confidence in him to solve his own problems.

The Outcome

When they first implement the safe space plan, it is tough. There is a lot of screaming and throwing things against the door. In anticipation of this, Charlotte and Kevin had replaced some of the toys that could be dangerous with a variety of rubber and foam objects that can be safely hurled, smashed, and stomped on. Still, they install the old video monitor back in his bedroom so they can be sure he is not in any real danger. Like most parents in similar situations, during the eye of the storm, Charlotte's and Kevin's worry is that separating from him in his time of distress is damaging to Alex. But they remind themselves of what the alternative looks like, which helps them stay the course.

After five minutes, Charlotte peeks through the opening that the "door helper" makes possible. Alex says he will be calm but then starts throwing foam balls at her, so she calmly lets him know that she sees he needs more time and that she'll be back in five minutes. When she returns, he asks for a bear hug. They sit quietly for a few minutes. Then, Alex says, "I don't know why I can't make my body behave." Charlotte acknowledges how distressing that must feel and points out that he actually did a great job of calming down in this instance: "You were in the 'red zone' and were able to get your mind and body calm again. I can see that feels so much better." She wants to reinforce Alex's belief that he can learn to soothe himself and to show she has confidence in him to be able to do just that.

Once the storm is over, Charlotte tells the story of what happened matter-of-factly. Recall that the trigger for the meltdown was Charlotte's asking Alex to be careful putting down his cup on the fragile glass table. He started shouting at her to stop using that word, "fragile," and then started kicking her. Charlotte recounts: "I asked you to be gentle when you put your cup down on the glass table because it is fragile and can break. You didn't like that I gave you this direction. You became very distressed and lost control of your words and your body." She pauses to give Alex time to respond. He doesn't say anything but he is calm and seems like he is taking this in. Charlotte then asks whether he thought she was angry at him or was criticizing him. He nods his head affirmatively. She tells him that people sometimes hear things in a way that the other person doesn't mean. She was just trying to be helpful—to give him information about what her expectation was. That is her job as a mom. She is going to help him feel more comfortable with accepting guidance because that is part of life. She reminds him that at school he is great at accepting and following the teacher's directions, and she is going to help him do this at home, too.

Regarding the soccer incident, in which Ellie blocked Alex's goal, Kevin recounts: "You kicked the ball. Ellie blocked it from going into the goal. That was frustrating and upsetting to you. You wanted to make a goal so badly. Your feelings were so big and overwhelming that you lost control and hit Ellie. Then, you decided to stop playing altogether."

Kevin is careful not to make statements like "No one is going to want to play with you if you hurt them or keep being a sore loser," or "You'll never get better at soccer if you keep quitting." He now sees that these types of responses increase Alex's feelings of shame and result in a defensive posture that doesn't help him work through his feelings.

Instead, Kevin helps Alex think through the natural outcome of his choices. He stays grounded in the mindset that he can't *make* Alex feel or act differently. Alex has to learn to look at his emotions and actions and decide to make changes. Kevin's responsibility is to guide Alex through this process—to let him know that he is not alone and that Kevin can handle Alex's most difficult feelings; that Kevin won't judge, shame, or punish him for his actions. He seeks to understand and support, not fix.

To this end, Kevin shows interest in understanding what the experience was like for Alex by asking questions, such as "What were you thinking and feeling when Ellie blocked the ball you were trying to kick into the goal?" "After you quit the game, what happened?" "How did you feel?" "What do you think the other kids were thinking?" "Is there a different way you would have liked it to have ended?" "How could you make that happen?" During this reflective process, Kevin is able to explain to Alex that being unkind with his words or actions is not just hurtful to the other child, it's not good for him, because it makes others have negative or uncomfortable feelings about him. That's why they are going to help him find other ways to express his feelings.

As for dealing with being aggressive toward other children, they explain to Alex that when he is having trouble controlling his body, it signals that it's time to take a break, which they will help him do. That might mean coming off the soccer field for a few minutes to cool down. They do this in a calm, supportive way. They don't shame or try to teach a lesson in that moment.

What about saying sorry? Charlotte and Kevin have found that trying to force Alex to say a mea culpa backfires. He resists it, which just results in another battle. (Note: Making a child say "sorry" falls into the category of things you *have no control over*. Trying to force it out of a child often results in the whole point of saying sorry being subjugated to the frustrating and ultimately useless power struggle. And, while a child may comply with the adult's direction to say "sorry," it is often to end the uncomfortable situation and is devoid of meaning.) Instead, Charlotte and Kevin brainstorm ways Alex can make it right. Saying "sorry" is one option. Other options might be offering a comforting gesture, dictating a note, or drawing a picture to give to the child. Choices reduce defiance.

As far as the safe space goes, it starts to yield positive changes. More often than not, Alex will accept a calming tool when he is starting to get agitated, and the need for the safe space is averted. And, now, when they have to take him to the safe space, sometimes they are able to stay with him; he may be screaming and thrashing but is not being physically aggressive. They sit with their backs to the door to create a boundary and stay perfectly quiet. They refrain from trying to calm him down because they have learned it only increases his agitation. Within a few minutes, Alex will often climb into their laps for a hug and sometimes even falls asleep.

Most importantly, Charlotte and Kevin are more positively connected to Alex. Now that they have a clear plan that enables them to maintain control when Alex is in the "red zone," they no longer feel like they are walking on eggshells. They are more relaxed and able to be their best selves with him—much more loving and responsive overall. And Alex is starting to be less reactive in situations that used to send him directly into the "red zone." The mantra and calming tools, more often than not, prevent the big meltdown.

WILL: THE BULL IN THE CHINA SHOP

Recall Will, the four-year-old sensory seeker who keeps getting into trouble for being aggressive with his body—slamming into others, hugging kids too hard, or pushing.

The Mindsets and Mindshifts

Once Tamisa and Brent see that it is a sensory processing challenge that is driving Will's behavior—something he currently has no control over—*they no longer see him as a bad kid who is disrespectful and misbehaving on purpose.* This enables them to put in place a plan to address the root cause of the problem as follows.

They show understanding and empathy about the driving force behind Will's aggressive actions. They now see that Will is not using his body in unsafe ways on purpose to hurt others, but that he craves these sensory experiences; pushing, smashing, and bumping up against things feel good to his body. His downstairs brain is driving him to meet these needs and overriding the functions of his upstairs brain.

They establish ways for Will to meet these sensory needs in more acceptable ways. When Will starts to seek intense sensory input in ways that are unsafe (smashing into objects) or uncomfortable to other people (body slamming or pressing his face hard against Tamisa's face), they guide him to meet that need using a range of tools, such as pulling stretch bands, jumping, squeezing him between couch bolsters, bouncing on a large exercise ball, pushing weighted balls, or doing wheelbarrow walking or jumping jacks, some of which can be used when outside the home too.

They use the safe space when necessary. In situations when Will is not able to accept an alternative and is having a hard time controlling his body, they use the safe space in the same, loving way that Charlotte and Kevin implement for Alex. They include a lot of sensory tools to calm himself in his safe space.

They arrange to have Will evaluated by an occupational therapist (OT). Given our collective sense that there is a significant sensory basis for Will's behavior, we agree that it is important to seek an evaluation by an OT. OTs can assess the underlying processes at work and address them using a play-based intervention that helps children's sensory systems process input in ways that enable them to better self-regulate and reduce challenging behaviors. Every county offers free evaluations and intervention services. (See information in the appendix.)

The Outcome

The OT assessment yields very important information about a range of challenges in Will's sensory processing system, including that he is underresponsive to sensory input, which is indeed the root cause of his sensory-seeking behavior. The therapy is extremely helpful in Will's ability to better regulate his body using a range of tools to meet his sensory needs in appropriate ways.

The OT, Tamisa, Brent, and I meet with Will's teachers to help them understand the root cause of Will's behavior and to come up with strategies for supporting Will at school. As a result, the teachers no longer see Will's behavior as "misbehavior." And now that they have tools to prevent Will's unsafe actions, they are able to be much more empathetic and loving toward him and to help him participate more positively in the classroom activities.

The same is true at home. Now that Tamisa and Brent understand the root cause of Will's behavior and see that he is not a bad kid (and they are not bad parents!), they feel much more positively toward him. The tools they now have to prevent or quickly deter potentially unsafe behaviors result in a sizable reduction in negative encounters and an increase in more pleasurable, loving interactions. Instead of having to end family movie night because Will is fiercely pressing his body into somebody or stomping his feet on the floor, to everyone's distraction, he sits in a wiggle seat and has a fidget—tools that provide the sensory input he needs in situations that are otherwise very sedentary and uncomfortable for Will. (See a list of sensory tools in the appendix.)

WHEN TO SEEK PROFESSIONAL HELP

Aggressive behavior is expected to some degree in early childhood given young children's lack of impulse control. But if the intensity and frequency of the aggressive behavior is interfering in your child's functioning—her ability to learn, explore, and engage in a healthy way at home and at childcare or preschool—as was the case with Will, it is time to consider seeking professional help. Talk to your child's health care provider or contact a child development specialist to do further evaluation to root out the underlying cause of the behaviors and to provide you with the tools and support to manage these challenging moments.

5

SLEEP

Tonya and Arthur report that bedtime with Jack, their four-year-old, has become a "nightmare." It's full of "two more stories, count to 100, sit there, snuggle here, look at my 'garden,' read another book, turn off the nightlight, no turn it back on, why does my finger hurt, how do you know it will feel better in the morning?" When they finally get Jack to climb into bed, he pops up because, oh no, his action figures are facing the wrong way on the shelf! The only way to get him to settle down is for Arthur to agree to lie down with Jack until he falls asleep because they don't want him waking up Chloe, his two-year-old sister, with whom he shares a room. She is a "total dream; two books, two songs, and she's out for the count." Tonya concludes, "This whole situation is starting to test my mental health."

It is the rare family that doesn't contend with some kind of sleep challenge in the early years. (If your baby slept through the night at six weeks or you have never had a kid who wouldn't stay in his bed after lights out, don't tell any of your friends or you'll have none.) If your child is like many I know, she will not go down without a fight. Few children happily send their parents off at bedtime; most want to extend their time with you as long as possible to forestall a separation from the people they love the most. Can you blame them? That's why setting and enforcing limits is almost always necessary for establishing healthy sleep habits. I'll say it again, what children want isn't always what they need.

Sleep issues, like other child-rearing challenges, are rarely resolved using a one-size-fits-all approach. Bedtime problems come in all shapes and sizes, and every child and family is different. That's why general prescriptions don't work; they don't consider the unique characteristics of each child and family. Cookie-cutter approaches often lead to more frustration for parents when the suggested plan does not feel comfortable for them or does not work for their child.

The biggest piece of the puzzle when it comes to sleep challenges, which prescriptive approaches rarely take into account, is your mindset. The lens through which you interpret and then react to nighttime issues often leads to unintended outcomes that not only don't solve the problem, but often exacerbate it. If you fear tantrums are harmful to your child, you are more likely to cave on limits that your child doesn't like, such as putting up a boundary to prevent him from coming out of his room repeatedly after lights out. If you see your child as being manipulative when he tries to draw you back into his room by calling out that he has just one more question to ask you or exclaiming that he needs just one more story and then PROMISES he will go to sleep, you are likely to react harshly, which only amplifies the power struggle around bedtime. Or, you focus on trying to force your child to fall asleep when you actually have no control over this physiological process. The more you insist that your child go to sleep, the more your child is motivated to fight closing her eyes to prove that you are not the boss of her.

It can be helpful to keep in mind that learning to sleep independently is a skill and learning any new skill entails some period of discomfort before we master it. None of us would have learned to swim if our parents had never taken off our floaties and allowed us to experience some sense of insecurity as we learned to take our first strokes on our own. The same is true when it comes to sleep. Most children experience some stress when learning this skill. But the only way to master it is by working through it so they can experience that, even though they *feel* they can't survive without a parent next to them helping them go to sleep, they *can* actually soothe themselves and are okay on their own. Note that research[17,18] shows that allowing children to learn to sleep on their own is growth-promoting "positive stress" and is not harmful. (See the appendix for a good piece on myths/facts about sleep training.)

To set and enforce the clear limits kids need to learn to sleep independently, you will need to keep reminding yourself that limits are loving, even in the face of your child's protests ("I don't feel safe! I'll never go to sleep if you don't lay with me!") and maybe some vomit (more on that later). This requires changing the voice in your head that tells you that it is harmful for your child to be unhappy or distressed at times. It is, in fact, a gift to help your child learn this important skill that leads to growth and resilience (not to mention, better and more sleep). Remember, one of the hardest and most confusing aspects of parenting is that sometimes what *feels* kind and loving is not what your child actually needs to thrive.

The stories below elucidate how changing your mindset can empower you to reduce sleep challenges and ensure everyone gets a good night's sleep. You will see that many of them entail establishing a boundary that prevents children from exiting their rooms after lights out (once the child is out of a crib). This intervention is understandably very uncomfortable for many parents, initially. The idea that they would have to secure their child in their room is not something they dreamed of when they became parents, but, by the time most families come to see me, they are ensconced in very tense battles with their children around bedtime. This includes children running out of their rooms repeatedly after lights out, which sometimes lasts for hours, and coming into their parents' bed in the middle of the night, disrupting everyone's sleep. Parents are exhausted and angry with their kids for causing so much stress. The bedtime routine that should be full of cuddles and connection has become fraught with tumult and tension. You will see from the following stories that, in these situations, putting up a clear and safe boundary is much more loving than the back-and-forth battles that ensue when children have free reign after lights out.

JACK: DELAY TACTICS

Thinking back to four-year-old Jack—the master of the delay tactic— several intersecting mindsets are getting in the way of Tonya and Arthur being able to implement better limits at bedtime.

The Mindsets and Mindshifts

For starters, like most parents, Tonya and Arthur *feel distressed when Jack is distressed. They are sure that the intensity of his screaming when they won't sing a 6th song or answer his 20th question at bedtime is harmful to him.*

Consequently, they feel very uncomfortable about sticking to a limit when he is flipping out.

They are also focusing all of their energy on *getting Jack to change his behavior,* to stop making so many demands and to quiet down and go to sleep so as not to wake up the baby. This mindset results in Tonya and Arthur giving in to each request, hoping that Jack will finally have had enough and will agree to go to sleep without a scream-fest. This places the outcome in Jack's hands. He is in charge.

At the same time, Tonya and Arthur are angry at Jack because *they feel he is manipulating them*—forcing them to give in to his demands. This results in a harsh, revved-up reaction that only amps up the power struggle.

Once we take a step back and analyze this dynamic, Tonya and Arthur see that it is the *lack of limits that is resulting in this negative spiral that is harmful to Jack.* They are able to look at the situation from a new perspective—that they are great parents who are doing a long, loving bedtime routine that is providing what Jack needs, despite his insistence that it's not enough. The likelihood that he is going to decide that he has had sufficient time with them and that they should go on about their evening business so he can get the sleep he needs is slim to none.

They also recognize that it is *not within their power to stop Jack from making demands or to be quiet. These are things they have no control over; it is Jack's mind and body, and only he can control what he says and does.* Further, *he is being strategic, not manipulative, in trying to get his way.* He is not doing anything deviant. His tactics are working, so he is sticking with them. It is up to Tonya and Arthur to change the rules of engagement around bedtime.

The Plan

Tonya and Arthur institute a five-minute "bedtime review" period after books each night. This gives Jack a set time to go through all the things he needs before lights out: water, potty, rearranging toys on shelves, and counting to 50. They use a visual timer so Jack can see exactly how much time he has for this process. They are clear that, once the timer goes off, they will say good night and see him in the morning.

They provide a tool for soothing himself when he has a hard time turning off. They tell Jack that he has a "memory place" in his brain where he can store all the things he still wants to talk with them about after lights out. In the morning, he can share all his thoughts and questions with them. (Providing a concrete tool for managing their thoughts and emotions can be very helpful and calming to children.)

They make a rule that there is no more noise allowed after lights out because it is quiet time in the house. They acknowledge that they can't actually make him do this—it's his voice and body, which only he controls. But, if he chooses to be noisy, they will move him to the guest room to sleep. Then, even if he makes a lot of noise, he won't wake up his sister. This is a limit they can actually enforce. (If you don't have a spare room, you can set up a safe sleep area in your bedroom for the child who is *not* having the problem. In this case, that would be Chloe. If a child knows that the fear of waking up a sibling is the key to getting into your room at bedtime, he will strategically continue to exploit that.) Jack actually loves sharing a room with Chloe, so being able to stay in the same room with her is an incentive.

They put together a bedtime box for Jack, with his help. It includes comforting objects like squishy balls and books—acceptable tools he can use to help soothe himself to sleep.

Finally, they role-play with Jack exactly how the plan will be implemented. They have him play out both choices: what happens when he quiets down at lights out and what happens when he is noisy and needs to go into the other room to sleep. They show him the gadget that will help him stay safe and secure in the guest room if he chooses to keep running out. (Role-playing is a great strategy whenever putting in place a new limit. It helps kids experience what the new plan will feel like, which they usually find very amusing. It also helps parents feel better equipped to actually implement the plan in the heat of the moment.)

The Outcome

The first night, it seems that all is going well until the timer goes off at the end of the "bedtime review" period. Jack starts back up with the litany of things he still needs to do. Tonya and Arthur remain calm. They remind Jack to store those things in his "memory brain." He's having none of it. They try to coax him into bed so they can tuck him in. He refuses and starts to make a big ruckus. Tonya and Arthur remind him of his choices: either to quiet down or go into the other room. They tell him they will put a timer on for one minute so he can think carefully about his decision. If he quiets down for the night once the timer goes off, he can stay. If he doesn't, they will take him to the other room. When the timer goes off, he says he'll be quiet, but, within seconds of their leaving the room, Jack is back up, jumping on his bed and singing at the top of his lungs.

Tonya goes back and simply asks whether Jack would like to bring any of his blankets or pillows to the other room to clearly communicate that she is not going to be drawn into a battle with him. They have explained the plan and are now implementing it. Jack refuses to take anything with him. (Tonya grabs a blanket and pillow, anticipating that he will change his mind when they get to the guest room, and wants to head off yet another power struggle.) Jack won't budge, so Tonya has to carry him. She says a loving good night, tells him she can't wait to see him in the morning, and leaves. They use a door helper to ensure Jack stays in the room. (They have placed a video monitor in that room so they can be sure he is safe.) He protests loudly, including a declaration that "it's illegal to ignore your child." (Both Tonya and Arthur are attorneys.) That gets them in the jugular; but they don't take the expected bait or let it derail them. After about 20 minutes, Jack falls asleep.

The next night, they go through the exact same steps before lights out. They remind Jack about his choices and give him a minute to think about whether he wants to sleep in his room with his sister or in the guest room. Having experienced that he can trust that his parents will implement the plan they have laid out—that his efforts to derail it are no longer working—he decides to stay quiet after lights out, and the bedtime battles are history. (By and large, kids are quick studies. Once they see that you mean what you say—that they can count on you to follow through with your plan, calmly and lovingly—they are better able to make good choices.) The icing on the cake is when Jack starts sharing at breakfast all the things that he has stored in his "memory brain."

LILY: FOOD AFTER LIGHTS OUT

Michael and Renata walk into my office and announce that they have a master manipulator living in their home. Every night after lights out, Lily, their three-year-old, calls to them insisting she is hungry and that she needs more food, despite the fact that dinner ended no more than an hour before bedtime. They go to her and tell her she had plenty of chances to eat before bed and that it's time to sleep. Lily is not convinced. She keeps at it with more desperation: "I will never be able to sleep if I don't have a yogurt right now!" Michael and Renata ultimately relent. As she eats, they are lecturing her about how there is no food after bedtime and this is the last night they are going to do this. But night after night, they are triggered by Lily's distress. What kind of parents are they if they refuse food to a hungry child? Their rational brains know this is not a healthy dynamic, but their worry that Lily is truly hungry is such a trigger for them that they give in every time—and then get angry at her for what they perceive as her putting them in this impossible situation. They have come to dread bedtime. To add insult to injury, one morning at breakfast, Lily announces to Michael: "Daddy, after you put me to bed tonight, I'm going to be reeeally hungry." (I love how she is able to come up with an effective strategy to get what she wants but she's not yet strategic about revealing her trade secret.)

The Mindsets and Mindshifts

When I talk with Michael and Renata about these encounters with Lily, they explain that, while they know in their heads that it is not a good idea to start feeding her after lights out, they feel extremely uncomfortable denying her food when she insists that she is hungry. It *feels "mean" and potentially harmful to withhold food*, regardless of how many opportunities they have given her to eat throughout the day. At the same time, they feel angry at Lily for manipulating them—taking charge of the bedtime routine, calling the shots. They focus all of their efforts on trying to get Lily to stop crying out for food so they don't find themselves in this difficult position anymore.

With these mindsets on the table, Michael and Renata are able to take an objective look at how their state of mind in these moments is affecting their ability to turn this situation around. Their first mindshift is that *Lily's behavior is strategic, not manipulative.* Her plan to access more food and more time with Mom and Dad after lights out is working, so she is sticking with it. She is doing exactly what her three-year-old brain dictates: to find ways to assert control over her world. Whatever tactics work are reinforced and go in the win column. They also see that *their goal of trying to get Lily to stop calling out for food after lights out is something they have no control over.* Waiting for her to give up this ritual means they are ceding the control to Lily and have no ability to establish a healthy bedtime routine. These mindshifts reduce Michael and Renata's anger and frustration and enable them to approach this situation more calmly, lovingly, and effectively.

The Plan

Michael and Renata make a clear plan for food options in the evening. They explain to Lily that dinner is the main meal. That is the time to fill her belly with what it needs to feel happy and full. Then, at book-reading time, they will offer her a small snack, such as fruit or cubes of cheese, which they call "last chance food." They explain that, after this snack, there is no more food until breakfast in the morning. (It is important that the snack they offer be small, not nearly enough to make up for dinner, so that she isn't motivated to just skip dinner altogether.) Offering another chance to eat before bedtime enables Michael and Renata to feel comfortable enforcing the no-food limit after lights out. They feel confident they have given Lily plenty of chances to fill her belly before bed.

They set a firm limit for what will happen after lights out. They tell her that they know they can't stop her from calling out for food after lights out. Only she controls what she says and does, but they are clear that they won't be responding. They will have given her lots of chances to eat before bed. If she chooses not to fill her belly and she is still hungry, she can have a big breakfast in the morning. They remind her that the great news is that she can always make a different decision the next night and eat more before bedtime. It's in her hands.

The Outcome

The first night when time for "last-chance food" rolls around, Lily, with an impish grin, rejects the offerings with a polite "Thanks, but I'm not hungry right now." Fifteen minutes later, and just three minutes after Mom and Dad have tucked her in, she is shouting that she isn't just hungry, she is *starving*. While every bone in their bodies tells them to bound upstairs with more food, Michael and Renata keep reminding themselves that this limit is loving, not mean. They are able to stay the course and not react.

They ultimately have to use a safety cover on the inside knob of Lily's door to prevent her from persistently running out of her room to try to continue pleading her case to them. As uncomfortable as this is for them, they see that Lily's ability to keep coming out is only getting her riled up more, which is not helpful or loving. It increases the intensity of the situation and makes it harder for her to calm down and cope with a reasonable limit.

After three nights of implementing this new approach, the protests cease. Lily has adapted to the new plan. Most importantly, they all enjoy a much more pleasant bedtime routine and end the day on a warm, positive note—the most important outcome.

MATTHEW: MIDDLE-OF-THE-NIGHT MENACE

Matthew, age two and a half, insists that his dada, Lewis, lie down with him every night until he falls into a deep sleep. He wants only Lewis, not Daddy (Peter, his other father). Lewis acquiesces night after night, even though both he and Peter have agreed that it is important for Matthew to fall asleep on his own.

Matthew also wakes up at some point in the middle of the night, every night, and crawls into bed with Lewis and Peter. They have tried all the usual strategies—rewards, bribery, and threats—to get Matthew to stay in his room all night, but none have worked. He puts up a huge fight and they cave. Their most recent incentive involved telling Matthew that they would buy him the superhero costume he has been pining away for as a reward (aka bribe) for staying in his bed all night. Matthew agrees to the plan in theory—he says he will stay in his room and is very excited about earning the costume.

But in practice, night after night, he continues to come into his dads' room between 2:00 and 3:00 a.m. He starts to plead with them to decouple getting the costume from having to stay in his room until morning, explaining, "I just can't do it!"

The Mindsets and Mindshifts

The biggest hurdle for Lewis and Peter is *the mindset that they are hurting Matthew by not letting him sleep with them. It feels mean to leave him all alone when he says he needs them.* It took them a very long time to find a surrogate to have Matthew. He was desperately wanted for so long, which makes it especially hard for them to do something that will make him unhappy.

The other stumbling block is that, to avoid the meltdown, *Lewis and Peter are focusing their efforts on trying to control Matthew*—to get him to agree to stay in his room all night. They are counting on his accepting the bribe or being swayed by a threat. When those tactics don't work, they find themselves frustrated and feeling totally perplexed as to what they can do to effect a positive change.

An additional challenge is that Matthew is playing preferences. Peter feels he is as warm and loving with Matthew as Lewis is. He is confounded by this new dynamic and is *angry and hurt at Matthew's rejection. He is taking it personally*, which is making it hard for him to stay calm and loving toward Matthew in these difficult moments. He often reacts by rejecting Matthew in return.

Taking a step back to look at the situation from an objective versus emotional lens, Lewis and Peter are able to see that *it is the current sleep scenario that is not healthy for Matthew*, or them for that matter. Everyone is tired and stressed. Learning to sleep on his own and for the whole night is what would be most loving for Matthew (and them!). *Just because Matthew doesn't like a limit, doesn't mean it's not good for him.* Importantly, this mindshift also means they *no longer live in fear of the tantrum*. This frees them to stop trying to get Matthew to change his behavior and instead put a system in place that puts them back in charge of implementing a healthier bedtime routine.

Following through with this also entails *not interpreting and reacting to Matthew's behavior at face value*. It is very common for children to play favorites. It doesn't mean that they love one parent more than the other. It is not always clear why children go through these stages. It is often situational; one parent is more available and acting as a primary caregiver, or one parent is the limit setter and the other more "lenient." Regardless of the reason, when the "rejected" parent takes it personally and responds with hurt and anger, it perpetuates the preference. Acting defensively is also confusing and overwhelming to the child since *he doesn't really mean to be hurtful*, which can further complicate his ability to move through this phase. With this insight, Peter is better prepared to mete out the plan they have developed. (For more on how to deal with parental preferences, see the appendix.)

The Plan

Lewis and Peter set a positive stage for the new bedtime system. They explain to Matthew: "Dad and daddy have been making big mistakes! What were we thinking? It turns out that our job is to make sure you get the sleep you need so that your mind and body grow healthy and strong. We haven't been doing a good job of that by letting you come into our bed every night. The doctor said it's really important for you to stay in your own bed so you can sleep more soundly and without interruption. So we are going to make a plan to help you see you are safe and secure in your room all night." (Parents taking the fall can be very effective in opening kids up to these kinds of discussions when making a change to the rules of engagement. Making the focus that you have messed up reduces children's natural defensiveness when they think they are going to be corrected.)

They stop using bribery. Lewis and Peter decouple getting the superhero costume from sleep. Not only is this strategy not working, but they see that using this carrot is just increasing Matthew's stress. They get him the costume to take that off the table.

They use "Bearbear," Matthew's lovey, as a support in the bedtime routine. They have Bearbear sit with them during book reading and encourage Matthew to point out the pictures to his lovey and explain the stories to him. Lewis and Peter tell Matthew that Bearbear needs Matthew to be his helper to go to sleep at bedtime. Putting Matthew in the role of authority and being an assistant is very appealing to him. (The more children associate their lovey with your nurturing family routines, the more powerful its ability to soothe them during separations and other stressful times.)

They decide that each parent needs a chance to have one-on-one time with Matthew. They explain to Matthew that Dada and Daddy will alternate nights lying down with Matthew for five minutes after lights out. Then, they will say good night and leave. They will use a visual calendar so Matthew can clearly see which parent will be with him for cuddle time each night.

They help Matthew create a bedtime box of soothing tools. Matthew can choose items that are calming and safe for him.

They make a recording of the three of them reading books together. They play it for Matthew when they leave the room. It serves as a "transitional object," a way to help him feel connected to them after they separate.

They establish a plan for what will happen after lights out. They explain that, once they leave the room, the parent who had laid down with him that night will come back one time to remind him that all is well. Just one time. They will do the same thing if he wakes up in the middle of the night. They create a mantra for these check-ins to provide a ritual that Matthew can count on. (I find that, more often than not, doing repeated check-ins is an obstacle to kids' falling asleep. If their parents keep returning, the child's energy gets focused on waiting for Mom or Dad to reappear, keeping them in a state of high arousal, when the goal is for them to be calming their minds and bodies to soothe themselves to sleep.)

They provide reasonable choices. After lights out, they will give Matthew two great choices. If he stays in his room, the door can remain open. If he chooses to come out, they will escort him back to his bed and use a door helper to help him stay in his room. They show him how this tool works so he knows exactly what to expect. They explain that they will take the door helper off once he is asleep. If he wakes up in the middle of the night and comes into their room, they will enact the same plan: they will escort him back to his bed and put up the door helper to help him stay in his room. At that point, the door helper will stay up for the remainder of the night. (They have a video monitor so they can see whether there is really anything wrong.)

Peter and Lewis present the plan in a very positive and upbeat, non-threatening tone. Think "We are so excited to help you be a great sleeper. You are going to have so many great choices in this plan!," not "Here is the new plan. If you don't cooperate and stay in your bed, we will put a lock on your door." (Children react as much to your nonverbal cues as to your words. Threats signal you are in for a fight and get kids' haunches up.)

The Outcome

When they tell Matthew about the new plan, as expected, there is a lot of protesting. He says he won't ever fall asleep without Dada next to him and he hates the monkey lock. He picks it up and tosses it down the hall. They calmly retrieve it and place it out of bounds. They are careful not to get derailed by Matthew's attempts to thwart the plan, which they are prepared for.

Accordingly, Lewis and Peter acknowledge Matthew's feelings and let him know that they don't expect him to like or agree with the plan, but they will be sticking to it because it is their job to help him see that he is safe and secure falling asleep on his own, and that he is capable of getting himself back to sleep in the middle of the night. (They are committed to following through with this plan because they are clear on the fact that it is Matthew's associating sleep with lying right next to Lewis that is a root cause of the challenges they are having in establishing a healthy bedtime routine for him and *for them*!)

Upon implementation, Matthew starts up as soon as Peter lies down with him for the five-minute cuddle time. He screams that he wants Dada. Peter acknowledges that Matthew would prefer Dada, whom he is used to lying down with at night. But the new plan is for each of them to have a turn cuddling with him. When Matthew continues to push Peter away, Peter remains calm and present. He tells Matthew that he has two choices: either Daddy can stay in the room with him until the five minutes are up or he can leave now, but Dada isn't coming in because it's Daddy's night. Matthew doesn't respond when Peter asks him whether he'd like Daddy to stay or go. He just pouts and turns his back to Peter. Peter stays in the room and starts to sing one of Matthew's favorite songs. He incorporates Bearbear into the singing. Matthew doesn't say anything, but he physically relaxes and starts to roll back to face Peter.

When Peter goes to kiss Matthew good night, Matthew gets grumpy again and shouts, "No kisses!" Peter, being responsive, not reactive, says: "No problem. I'll blow you a kiss from the door. Love you, sweet boy. Now, Bearbear, remember that Matthew is here to help you get to sleep. He will keep you safe. That's his job." And he leaves.

Matthew stays in his room but repeatedly shouts that he needs Dada to come back in for another kiss. Peter goes to Matthew's door after about five minutes and says his mantra: "We love you, bud. We can't wait to see you in the morning. Sleep tight." After about 15 minutes, Matthew's protests start to wane. They can hear him saying to Bearbear, "It's okay; I hold you." Matthew eventually falls asleep after about 30 minutes.

In the middle of the night, Matthew awakens and calls out for Dada, but he doesn't come out of the room. Peter goes to Matthew's doorway, whispers the mantra, and goes back to bed. Matthew continues to shout for Dada on and off for about 20 minutes, but he eventually falls back to sleep.

Over the next several nights, a similar scenario unfolds. Matthew continues to call out for Dada, but this decreases in length and intensity. They never need to use the door helper because Matthew never actually comes out of the room. He often goes to the transom but never crosses that boundary. Each morning, to underscore that Matthew survived the new plan, Peter and Lewis tell him that he did a great job getting himself to sleep and staying in his room until morning. That is the key—to help Matthew change his narrative around bedtime; to see that, while he thought he couldn't sleep without Dada next to him, he now has lived experience that, indeed, he can. When he wakes up each morning, he sees that all is still right with the world.

By the fourth night, the new bedtime routine is solidified, and everyone is much happier for it. And, as Peter stays the course—not reacting to Matthew's rejection—the parental preference stage starts to abate as well.

ELLIOT: NIGHTMARE NIGHTMARES

Elliot, age three and a half, has started to get up in the middle of the night saying he had a bad dream. He comes into his mom Angie's room and wants to sleep with her. All efforts to coax him back to his bed result in hysterics so she lets him stay in her bed. Angie wants to be sensitive to his fears, but, as a single mom, Elliot's awakening at night and insisting on sleeping in her bed is interfering big time in her ability to function at full capacity during the day. He moves around all night, making it impossible for either of them to get any rest. She feels stuck as to how to support Elliot without enabling him.

The Mindsets and Mindshifts

Angie is in a very tough position. *It feels so wrong and rejecting not to allow Elliot to sleep with her when he is afraid.* (Few parents feel comfortable leaving a child alone when he says he is scared.) At the same time, she is concerned about setting a pattern, especially because this current dynamic is resulting in sleep deprivation for both of them, which has its own set of negative consequences.

As we take a step back to think about what Elliot *needs* (vs. wants) from Angie to feel safe and no longer afraid at night, Angie gains a new perspective and makes an important mindshift. *While allowing Elliot to stay in her bed feels like the best and most supportive response, doing so inadvertently confirms for Elliot that there is, in fact, something to be afraid of and that he is okay only if Angie is with him—that he is not safe on his own.* Essentially, *what he wants is not what he needs.* Fears are a part of life. Helping Elliot manage his fears and not depend on Angie to take them away is a gift, because the only way children (or any of us) get over fears is by living through them and experiencing that they are unfounded. For example, a child finally goes down the big slide he was terrified of and sees that he survived; or a child makes it through and thrives by the end of the first week of preschool after screaming for dear life not to be left in this strange, scary place. These children have developed greater resilience.

At nighttime, the same rules apply; children need to experience that the fears in their heads are not real and they are okay on their own. We don't want to set kids up to think that they can't handle these feelings and that they can cope only if you are with them. We want to empower our kids with the tools and confidence to master these fears. This is very important for Angie to keep in mind because, if she thinks that she is harming Elliot by not physically being with him as he works through his fears, it will be impossible to follow through with any plan that entails setting limits and boundaries around sleep. (This is another example where what kids need is completely counterintuitive to what *feels* right—the positive parenting paradox.)

The other factor that Angie suspects is at play is that Elliot has put two and two together; saying that he had a bad dream results in a lot of attention in the middle of the night and lands him a spot in her bed—his preference. She is afraid this dynamic is taking on a life of its own and is very worried about the negative impact the disruption in sleep is having on both of them.

Making the mindshift that *continuing to rescue Elliot won't help him get over his fears, nor will it lead to a healthy night's sleep, and that helping Elliot feel safe in his own room is loving, not harmful*, Angie is ready to make a new plan.

The Plan

Angie teaches Elliot about a tool for managing his fears: his "worry" versus "thinking" brain. She explains that we all have a "worry" brain that makes us think we are in danger from monsters or ghosts. We also have a "thinking" part of our brain that helps us know whether or not something is real. Sometimes, our worry brains trick us into thinking we need to be afraid of something when actually we're totally safe, like when he is afraid that Mommy might not return from a work trip, even though she always comes back. Making it about their brains helps children process and make sense of their complex feelings. It makes the feelings more manageable.

Angie includes time in their bedtime routine to go through the list of Elliot's worries and helps him use his thinking brain to problem solve. He doesn't like it pitch black, so she puts a night-light in his room. They go through his room together to show him there is nothing scary lurking around. Since he is afraid of something coming in through his window, Angie shows him how it shuts tight and can be locked. (Some parents spray a special potion [water] around the room and use other strategies like this to keep monsters and other scary things at bay. The risk of these kinds of solutions is that they suggest that monsters do exist, which can lead to confusion for children if we are also trying to help them understand that these fears are not real.)

She integrates Elliot's lovey, "Bunny," into their bedtime routine. She suggests that Bunny might like to sit on Elliot's lap while they are reading and cuddle with them when singing lullabies. Angie then puts Elliot in the role of being a protector for Bunny. She suggests that Bunny might need Elliot's help to feel safe at night, so he might want to explain to Bunny that the scary things are in his worry brain. This puts Elliot in the driver's seat and in a mindset that he is the strong, capable one who can keep his lovey safe.

They brainstorm ways that Elliot can soothe himself when he wakes up in the middle of the night: singing himself or his lovey a favorite song or hugging a memory foam pillow—something many children find very soothing. Empowering him with tools for calming himself helps him feel in control and able to take care of himself. (See the appendix for a list of calming tools for kids.)

Using a digital audio device, Angie records them reading books and singing bedtime songs together. When Angie puts Elliot to sleep at night and/or when he wakes up in the middle of the night, she plays the recording as a tool to help him cope with being separated from her.

Angie creates a plan for exactly what will happen if Elliot wakes up in the middle of the night. If he wakes from a bad dream, he can call on his thinking brain to reassure his worry brain that the fears aren't real, and remind himself of all the soothing tools he can use to calm himself. She explains that if he comes into her room in the middle of the night, she'll walk him back to his room and reassure him that all is well. She'll remind him about his worry versus thinking brain and about all his soothing tools. She will turn on the audio recording but is clear that she will do that only one time, even if he calls out for her to put it on again. He can listen to it as much as he wants in the morning. (Note that, while these kinds of recordings work well for some children, for others, it becomes more fodder for a power struggle. Use your judgment; you know your child best.)

As for what Angie's plan will be if Elliot keeps coming back into her bedroom, she decides she will cross that bridge when she gets to it. Right now she does not feel comfortable putting up a boundary at his door.

Angie role-plays the plan with Elliot. She has him pretend he has had a bad dream or has awakened feeling afraid in the middle of the night. She prompts him to call out to her or to come to her room. Then, she plays out the process—walking him back to his room and reminding him of his worry versus thinking brain and all of his calming strategies. Practicing the plan lets Elliot experience exactly what to expect.

The Outcome

The first night Angie implements the plan is difficult. Elliot keeps coming out of his room and trying to climb back into her bed. She and I have a call to problem-solve this. Angie still doesn't want to put a boundary at Elliot's door, so we come up with an alternative: Angie will set up a space on the floor of her room with some blankets and a pillow where Elliot can sleep. Angie is aware that this will still reinforce Elliot's perception that he needs to be next to her to be safe at night, but it solves the problem of her sleep being interrupted.

Angie explains this new plan to Elliot: if he awakens in the night, he can come into her room and sleep in the space she has created for him, but he can't wake her up. That works for a few nights. But then Elliot starts insisting on climbing back into her bed. At this point, Angie decides to use a gate at his door. This feels really uncomfortable to her, but the current state of affairs is so debilitating that she feels ready to pursue a new path.

The first night Angie escorts Elliot back to his room and uses the gate, he bangs on it and shouts for her. Angie calls to him from her room periodically to reassure him. In a soothing voice she says, "You're okay, sweetie. We are all safe. I love you and can't wait to see you in the morning." After about 30 minutes, Elliot falls asleep at the base of the gate and sleeps until morning. At breakfast, Angie makes a big deal about how Elliot's thinking brain prevailed over his worry brain and emphasizes how he has slept safely in his room on his own. She also reminds Elliot that if he doesn't like having the gate up at night, he can choose to stay in his room; then there's no need for the gate. If he needs reassurance, instead of coming into her room, he can call to her and she will repeat the mantra to remind him that everything is okay.

The next night, Elliot still comes into her room at around 2 a.m. Angie calmly escorts him back to his room, says her loving mantra, puts the gate up, and goes back to bed. Elliot protests, but for less time, and there is no banging on the gate. The following night, he just calls out to her in the middle of the night, and Angie says her mantra. He asks her to say it one more time. She does. Elliot then goes back to sleep. Within a few more days, Elliot is sleeping through the night. Each morning, Angie is sure to reinforce the important message "You were afraid. Your worry brain was in charge last night for a little bit. But your thinking brain reminded you that you are safe, and you got yourself back to sleep. Now, it's morning, and you see that everything is fine—just the way it always is." They also talk about which tools he used to calm himself to reinforce their helpfulness.

This plan proves so effective that Angie continues to use the concept of the worry and thinking brains for Elliot's other fears. She is amazed to see how resilient he can be—how much stronger his coping skills are than she ever imagined. (This is a very important insight: our own anxiety about our children's fears often leads us to jump to the rescue. We worry that our kids can't handle their fears, when in fact they are often much more resilient and competent than we think they are. We need to trust that they can master their fears and give them the chance to do so, with support, just like Angie's plan provided.)

While dealing with your children's fears can be very triggering, these are some of the most powerful opportunities to positively shape your children's development. You are helping them feel confident that they can cope with the other challenges they will face as they grow.

BELLA: WHO'S THE BOSS?

Five-year-old Bella is a force. She is bright, sensitive, and feisty. She knows what she wants and will go to great lengths to pursue her goals. She has a very intense need to be in control. Recently, when she asked her mom, Nikki, if she could watch another episode of her favorite TV show, Nikki responded that Bella could have more screen time after she cleaned up her toys. Bella's response: "Mom, I am just so exhausted from being bossed around all the time."

Bella's pursuit of control is next level at bedtime, especially since the advent of COVID-19. It has been hard for Bella to accept that, even though Mommy and Daddy (Jim) are home now during the day, they can't play. They need to be in a quiet space to work and Bella is not allowed to interrupt them. Grandma is in charge while Mom and Dad work. Jim has a few windows to connect with Bella throughout the day, whereas Nikki's job allows very little room for breaks. So the reading and cuddle time Nikki has at bedtime is very special for her and Bella.

But, now, bedtime has gone off the rails. Bella insists that Nikki stay in bed with her until she falls asleep. When Nikki thinks Bella is down for the count, she quietly gets up to leave, but Bella pops up and says, "No, Mommy, I'm not asleep yet. Lie back down!" This can go on for hours. Nikki is angry at Bella for being so demanding and manipulative, and for putting Nikki in what she sees as a no-win situation. She feels like a hostage.

Further, this nightly scenario results in Bella not falling asleep until way too late, between 9:30 and 10:00 p.m., a full hour after the time Nikki and Jim feel is healthy for her. But Nikki's fear of "ruining" the limited, one-on-one time they have together makes setting any limits very challenging.

The Mindsets and Mindshifts

As we analyze this situation, the mindset that is front and center for Nikki is that *it feels mean and rejecting not to stay with Bella* at night until she is ready for Nikki to leave, especially because of the limited time she has with Bella during the day. Nikki's own mother worked constantly when she was a child. Many days, Nikki didn't see her at all. Nikki has made a firm commitment to be sure to spend a lot of quality time with her children, to have a strong relationship with them and to meet their emotional needs. She worries that *the distress Bella experiences when Nikki tries to extricate herself at bedtime is harmful to Bella and worries that she will feel abandoned. At the same time, feeling that Bella is controlling her through her demands—being manipulative—makes Nikki uptight and preoccupied throughout the bedtime routine in anticipation of the prolonged power struggle to come at lights out.*

Nikki recognizes that the negative feelings she is having about Bella are putting a damper on the whole bedtime routine that is so special to them. This realization, combined with the worry about the negative effects of reduced sleep for Bella, leads to an important mindshift that *it would actually be more loving for Bella, not mean or harmful, to set limits around bedtime.*

Looking at the situation objectively also helps Nikki see that *Bella is just being strategic—an attribute she values highly and wants to nurture in Bella—not "manipulative."* There is nothing wrong with her trying to get Nikki to stay in bed with her. It is up to Nikki and Jim to set the appropriate limits around bedtime and beyond so that behaviors they don't think are healthy for Bella are not reinforced. They both see that the balance is too often tipped to giving Bella more power than is appropriate. They recognize the importance of finding a way to give Bella choices and agency, and to be loving, connected parents, while staying in charge.

The Plan

Nikki commits to being more present with Bella. She identifies two periods during each workday when she can have uninterrupted time with Bella. It might be 20 minutes for lunch and 15 minutes for play or book-reading. Nikki also commits to putting her phone and laptop away from dinnertime through the bedtime routine with Bella. She knows she will feel more comfortable setting limits with Bella when Nikki has had time to connect with Bella during the day.

Nikki and Jim create more boundaries around the bedtime routine. Instead of reading books in the family room after Bella has had a bath and brushed her teeth, they decide to do book reading in her bedroom to reduce the number of transitions Bella has to make right before bed. Moving Bella directly from the bathroom to her room also prevents her from getting into overdrive, racing up and down the halls and getting more wound up at a time when she needs to start to calm her body for sleep.

Once in her room, they read two stories together as a family. Jim, then, says his good night. The routine concludes with Bella and Nikki having their cuddle time. Nikki lets Bella choose which alarm sound on

Mom's phone will signal that snuggle time is over and that it's time for Nikki to say good night and leave the room. They create a mantra that Nikki says every night as she tucks Bella in: "Good night, sleep tight. I can't wait to see you in the morning."

They teach Bella about her thinking and worry brains. Nikki and Jim explain the worry and thinking brain concept (like Angie did for Elliot). They tell Bella that while her worry brain may be telling her that she is not okay unless Mom is in the room with her until she falls asleep, her thinking brain can remind her that she does so many things on her own and that she can do this too. Bella responds very positively to this idea, that there are parts of her brain that she can control, because, after all, she is all about control right now. They also tell Bella that her lovies (two stuffed puppies) need her help to use *their* thinking brains to know that they are safe and sound. They are counting on Bella to take good care of them through the night.

They establish a clear plan for what will happen after lights out. They tell Bella that she has two great choices: if she stays in her room after Nikki leaves, the door can stay open. If she comes out of the room, Jim will escort her back in, without any talking or interaction, and close the door. (We decide it's better for Jim to play this role because they believe he is less triggering to Bella when it comes to bedtime. Her association with needing Mom to go to sleep is so strong that continued interaction with Nikki after lights out will make it harder for Bella to settle down.) If she continues to come out, Daddy will keep bringing her back to her room. Nikki and Jim are clear that it is their job to make sure she stays safely in her room all night and they are going to do that. (Nikki and Jim don't want to use a tool that would prevent Bella from opening up her door and repeatedly exiting her bedroom. They want to first see if they can execute the plan without erecting this boundary. They agree that if that doesn't work, they will place a safety cover on the doorknob to ensure they can implement the important limit Bella needs and to prevent the situation from escalating further. They remind themselves that she was in a crib until age three and they had no problem with that; she was safe and secure and could not exit her room then. This is an important mindshift—that boundaries are loving, not mean or harmful.)

The Outcome

When Nikki and Jim present the new plan to Bella, they start by telling her that they are in big trouble with her pediatrician, Dr. Ellen, again! Invoking Dr. Ellen in the past around other behavioral challenges has been a very effective tool. Most recently, when they were concerned about Bella's habit of standing too close to the TV, they explained to Bella that Dr. Ellen had said Mommy and Daddy were making a big mistake by letting Bella do this because it isn't good for her body. Dr. Ellen said she should be at least eight big steps away. Bella had responded enthusiastically to this idea that her parents were in trouble with the doctor, which she found very humorous. This put her in a more open state of mind about changing her behavior. Now, every time she watches TV, she takes eight dramatic steps back.

Nikki and Jim explain that this time they are in trouble with Dr. Ellen because it turns out that mommies and daddies are not supposed to stay with five-year-olds until they fall asleep, because kids this age are capable of getting themselves to sleep on their own. And, when Mommy is in the bed with her, it makes Bella stay up too late. Dr. Ellen says that this is not good for Bella's brain or her body, which need a lot of rest at night to grow strong. So that's why they have made this new bedtime plan.

Nikki and Jim can see that Bella is torn about this. She is very interested in Dr. Ellen's perspective, but she is not keen on the new plan. They acknowledge her disagreement and displeasure, but clearly explain that they are going to follow through with it because it is their job. They need to be the best mommy and daddy they can be and be sure Bella has a chance to fall asleep at an earlier, healthier time. They also remind Bella that she has done so many other new things that felt hard at first until she saw she was totally capable of handling these challenges. They share some recent examples of fears she has faced and muscled through.

As for the specifics of the plan, Bella loves the idea that she is the caretaker for her puppies, and she likes choosing the alarm on Mom's phone to signal the end of cuddle time; but, no surprise, when the alarm sounds and Nikki starts to get up, Bella insists that Mommy has to stay. She needs more time with her. She won't sleep if Mommy doesn't stay.

Nikki stays calm and loving. She reminds Bella that her thinking brain knows she can fall asleep on her own and that her puppies need her now. She says the mantra and then leaves. Bella chases after her. Jim takes over at this point (while Nikki gets as far away as possible and distracts herself to avoid running to the rescue). He walks Bella back to her room. She shouts that she will never get into bed unless Mommy comes back. Jim acknowledges that it is a big change to not have mommy fall asleep next to her and that he understands she isn't happy about the new plan, but they are still going to implement it to help her see she is safe on her own. He tells Bella that he is going to close the door, as they had discussed; but that if she comes out again, he is going to use a special doorknob cover that prevents her from being able to open the door to be sure she stays safely in her room. He shows it to her and demonstrates how it works. He also has her test it out. He presents this matter-of-factly, not as a threat. He is just helping her know exactly what to expect. He stays calm and loving throughout, which he is able to do only because he knows that providing this boundary is helpful and that the emotionally charged back-and-forth with Bella is what is harmful for her. Nikki, meanwhile, is trying to divert herself as she listens to this exchange from afar. She has to take a lot of deep breaths and keep reminding herself that, while this whole process feels mean, setting clear boundaries that will help Bella learn that she is capable of sleeping on her own is a gift.

Bella says she doesn't want the doorknob cover and will stay in her room if Daddy will leave the door open. Jim agrees, but Bella comes bounding back out. He walks her back in, calmly puts the cover on the doorknob and says goodnight. Bella shouts at the door for Nikki. Jim and Nikki swing past her room periodically to say their mantra through the door but they don't go back in and they don't linger. After about 20 minutes, they hear Bella climb into bed and start talking to her puppies about their thinking brains and telling them they are safe and everything is going to be okay. The second night, they remind Bella about the plan and exactly what to expect: if she stays in her room at lights out, the door can stay open. If she comes out, they will use the doorknob cover as a helper. She says she still hates the door helper and wants it to go away. They respond that the great news is that it is in her hands. If she doesn't want the door helper, she can always stay in her room. At lights out, she comes running out again. Jim calmly walks her back to her room. She begs him not to put the door helper on. He says that there is no need for the door helper if she chooses to stay in her room and he will give her a chance to make a different decision. (This can be a slippery slope; you don't want to give too many chances, or that starts to take on a life of its own. Two chances can quickly turn into 10, but giving your child an opportunity for a redo one time can be effective.) In this case, Bella does choose to stay in her room. By the third night, Bella keeps calling out for Nikki for a good half hour after Nikki says good night, but she stays in her room. Nikki sticks to the plan, calling out the mantra to assure Bella that she is still there and everything is okay. Nikki does not return to re-engage in the unhealthy dynamic.

Despite following this exact plan night after night, Bella continues to call out for Nikki at lights out for two more weeks. By week three, Bella calmly gets herself to sleep without her bids for Mom to come back. (Fierce children are very persistent. One child I recently worked with continued to scream at the top of his lungs for five minutes before falling into a deep sleep for a full month after his parents had implemented a clear and loving plan that they adhered to, to the letter. Then, on night 33—but who's counting—he just climbed into bed and went to sleep. Each child has his own path.)

Working through this challenge with Bella, which yielded such a good outcome, helps Jim and Nikki begin to feel much more comfortable setting appropriate limits with her across the board. Seeing that instituting clear, age-appropriate boundaries is not being dictatorial or mean and is not eroding Bella's sense of agency or competence, results in a major, positive mindshift for Nikki and Jim. It empowers them to apply a similar approach to other power struggles they have with Bella around mealtime and cleanup. This change in the family dynamic enables them to feel and respond more lovingly toward Bella. And, they no longer live in fear of the protest or tantrum—a major relief.

SOLUTIONS TO COMMON SLEEP CHALLENGES

Following are some sleep scenarios that many families who seek my help struggle with and are especially triggered by. Faulty mindsets abound that make it hard for parents to work through these bumps in the road in a way that helps their children develop healthy sleep habits. The most prevalent and powerful is the belief that it is harmful to their child to let him struggle to solve a problem. They feel compelled to make it all better to relieve their child's distress. In fact, I find, over and over again, that once parents set a clear and appropriate limit, children are incredibly competent at either solving the problem at hand (i.e., finding the lost binky or getting their blankets just the "right" way) or adapting to not getting what they want but really don't need.

Your child throws up from crying. The super feisty kids are often the ones who will vomit from crying when their parents set a limit at bedtime. Talk about triggering behaviors; for most parents, this is a 10 out of 10 on the stressor scale. (I have talked to many pediatricians about this behavior, and they assure me that it is not inherently harmful for an otherwise healthy child who is in a safe and secure family environment to throw up when upset.) Most parents respond by giving in on whatever limit they were trying to set, such as having their child fall asleep without a parent lying next to him or not allowing their child to sleep in their bed. While this may sound heartless, I find the best way to eliminate this behavior, which is certainly not healthy for the child, is to give it as little attention as possible. Quietly and gently change your child's clothing and put her back in bed with minimal engagement. This prevents her from associating vomiting with interaction. If you make a big deal about it and bring her into your bed or lay down with her, she puts two and two together and, voilà, the vomiting is reinforced as a successful strategy for engaging you. This goes in the category of things that feel mean but are actually loving. It can be very helpful to tell your child in advance what the plan will be: "Sometimes, when Daddy won't come back to tell you more stories after he says goodnight, you get so upset that you throw up. When that happens, we will help you get cleaned up. But, remember, after lights out it is nighttime, which is for sleep. That's the time for our brains and bodies to be quiet and get recharged. Daytime is for talking, playing, and interacting. So after lights out we won't be talking or playing or telling more stories. We will get you cleaned up and then we will see you in the morning when we'll tell lots of stories and have lots of time to talk and play together, again." This shows your child respect by telling him exactly what to expect. Sometimes it reduces or eliminates the behavior altogether because naming it and showing that you aren't worried about it diffuses its power.

Your child throws his lovey (or binky) out of the crib and then screams for it. It is the rare parent who is not going to feel incredibly mean by refusing to keep retrieving the lovey and handing it back to his or her child. But, if your child knows that this tactic will result in your returning to her after lights out, it confirms this as a successful strategy and is thus reinforced. Further, it keeps the engagement going—increasing your child's arousal level—at a time when she needs to calm her mind and body. That is not helpful to her.

Let your child know that she has two great choices: if she keeps her lovey in bed with her, she gets to have lovey with her all night; if she chooses to throw lovey out, she will have lovey in the morning. If it's the binky that your child is hurling, attach a basket on the side of the crib that your child can access so he has several binkies at his disposal. If he chooses to throw them all out of the crib, he can have them in the morning.

It's helpful to ask yourself what the alternative is in these situations. It is short-term pain for long-term gain. Remember, children learn to make good choices by experiencing the outcomes of their actions. Few children will keep throwing their lovey out if they know they won't get it back until morning.

Your child has an endless list of tasks he insists on doing before he can go to sleep. Just when you think he is satisfied, he conjures up one more task. In this case, I suggest baking into the bedtime routine a few minutes during which your child can organize things the way he likes them. When time is up, it's lights out and you leave. If he is really desperate to make more changes, he is free to do that on his own. You can't stop him, unless he's still in a crib. The key is that it no longer serves as a delay tactic. Miraculously, the desperation to do more organizing often evaporates when it no longer results in parental attention.

Your child gets really wound up right before bed. She runs out of the bathroom after bath/toothbrushing and becomes a whirling dervish. This leads to most parents getting revved up and frustrated. They engage in all sorts of strategies to get their kids to calm down and into their bedroom. They coax/cajole, threaten, offer bribes/ rewards, all of which only increases the child's dysregulation as it becomes a big chase game.

The antidote: don't enable an opportunity for your child to go into overdrive. Like Nikki and Jim did with Bella, make a clear rule in your routine that you go straight from the bathroom to the bedroom. Close the door to provide a boundary as you do your book reading. Dim the lights to create a soft, soothing atmosphere to help your child's mind and body quiet down. This prepares her to get herself to sleep when it's time for lights out.

I have also found that starting the book reading while your child is still in the bath can be a very helpful strategy. Your child picks out a book before getting into the tub. Bath time ends with your reading the book halfway through. Insert a bookmark your child has made, then finish it when you get into her room. This creates a bridge from bath to bed and makes the transition easier, as your child looks forward to hearing the rest of the book.

Your child insists he has to go to the potty after lights out, even after you have given him many opportunities to do so right before you say good night. This is a tricky one, as understandably, most parents feel very uncomfortable with the idea of not allowing their child to relieve himself, even if they are pretty certain it's a delay tactic. If your child can independently use the toilet, then let him know he is free to use it on his own. For children who are not yet able to go through the process by themselves, the best solution I have found is to put a kiddie potty in your child's bedroom. You tell your child that after lights out, if he needs to go, that is the potty he can use. You will help him clean it out in the morning. In most cases, the child never actually uses or needs it because he really doesn't have to go. Either way, this is a loving and effective solution, as it puts the control in your child's hands and eliminates unnecessary power struggles.

Your child wakes up super cranky in the morning or after naptime. Like Maggie, whom you met in chapter 2 on cooperation, the minute you enter your child's room, she is shouting at you to go away. Then, as soon as you leave, she is screaming for you to come back. The more you try to coax or cajole your child into a better mood, the more irritable she becomes. You feel mean for leaving her when she is distressed. You also feel helpless to control her and get her to calm down.

While this is the last thing you need when you are trying to get a positive start to your day, it's important to keep in mind that your child is not making mornings miserable on purpose. Some children (and adults) have a harder time making what are called "state changes," which means going from awake to asleep and asleep to awake. Their bodies are more reactive. These physiological transitions are uncomfortable for them. It takes them more time to settle their bodies to sleep and feel clear-headed and calm upon awakening. Here are some strategies families have found useful for helping their children adjust to the new day in a loving way:

- **Create a wake-up ritual.** Rituals are very calming and regulating for kids. For example, you might include an additional book at bedtime that you read halfway through. You can make it a math activity by helping your child count how many pages are in the entire book and then identify what page marks the middle. Have your child make a bookmark that she can place at that midpoint of the book. In the morning, when she wakes up, you enter the room, turn the lights on low (some parents wear a headlamp or use a flashlight), and finish the book by her bedside. Another option is to put on an audiobook for your child when she wakes up.
- **Give your child a sense of control.** Even if your child has called out for you, it can be overstimulating for her to start engaging right away. These sensitive kids can feel bombarded, even if you are being quiet and gentle. Your entry signals that it is time to start the day, which neither their mind nor their body is ready for. Calmly and lovingly tell your child that you see she needs more time to wake up. Leave the room and wait for her to provide a cue that she is ready for you to come back in. It might be saying a silly mantra, singing a favorite tune, or just calling out, "I'm ready!" Another strategy is to just enter the room and sit quietly with your child without making any demands. You whisper that you see that she still needs some time to wake up. No problem. You will give her time. She should just let you know when she's ready. Giving her some space might be all she needs to pull herself together.

- **Create a wake-up box for your child.** Put it together with him. Include things that are soothing to your child, like squishy objects, stuffed animals, or books. Let him know that this is his special box for when he wakes up from a nap or in the morning. He can use it if he needs time to himself before Mommy or Daddy comes to get him.

Your child wakes up in the middle of the night. I suggest going through the same steps you used at bedtime. Repetition enhances learning and builds new associations. When your child awakens and calls for you in the middle of the night, pop your head in one time, say the mantra, and leave. If you do this consistently, your child comes to associate the mantra with your love and serves as a reminder that all is well. I discourage going back in repeatedly because most children get very focused on waiting for their parents' return instead of calming themselves back to sleep.

If your child is waking up and saying she is afraid or that she has had a nightmare, the story about Elliot in this chapter lays out a loving approach that helps children cope with their fears in the middle of the night. It involves: talking to your child about her thinking versus worry brain; including time in your bedtime routine to go through your child's worries and help her use her thinking brain to problem solve; incorporating your child's lovie into the plan as a source of support; providing calming objects for self-soothing; letting your child know exactly what the plan will be in the middle of the night—that you will check in one time to provide reassurance and to remind her thinking brain that she is safe and secure; and finally role-playing the plan so your child knows exactly what to expect.

GUIDING PRINCIPLES FOR ESTABLISHING HEALTHY SLEEP HABITS

Following are a series of guiding principles that can help you avoid getting stuck in faulty mindsets that become obstacles to helping your child get a good night's sleep while maintaining strong, positive family relationships.

It's all about associations. If children associate falling asleep with being fed, held in someone's arms, rocked, or with someone lying right beside them—like many of the children in the stories above—they come to depend on these experiences to doze off. In the middle of the night, when they wake up due to natural sleep cycle fluctuations, they need the parental support they are used to in order to fall back to sleep. Changing these associations means going through a period of discomfort until the child experiences that he can fall asleep on his own. That is why the key to an effective strategy is often having the parent with whom the child has a less strong association around sleep carry out the plan. That parent would be the one to read the final book, be the last to leave the room at lights out, and deal with the middle-of-the-night awakenings.

Less is more. When devising a sleep strategy, keep in mind that, the more you emotionally and physically engage with your child after lights out, the harder it will be for her to soothe herself to sleep. Any kind of interaction is stimulating and increases children's arousal at a time when they need to feel calm.

That's why incremental approaches often backfire, for example, sitting by the child's bed and then each night moving the chair further back until the parent is out of the room. I find more often than not that this approach increases stress for both the child and the parent. Having Mom or Dad in the room presents a major stimulus for children, who naturally keep bidding for their parent's attention. This often leads to exactly the situation the parent is trying to avoid: getting into a heated back-and-forth, chock full of pleading and threats, to get his or her child to settle down.

I find that it is generally more helpful to children when you just peek into the room and whisper a loving mantra from the doorway to provide reassurance ("Good night, sleep tight, everything is alright, I love you") and then leave. When you engage in a more interactive way after lights out, especially in the middle of the night, it not only increases your child's arousal—it confuses him. Kids do best when expectations are clear: daytime is for interaction, such as talking, playing, and cuddling, and nighttime is for sleep—the time when bodies and minds need to be quieted and calm in order to grow big and strong. It will feel awful when he starts crying out for you to come back. How could it not? That's when you have to keep reminding yourself that, while he wants connection with you, engagement at this time is not helping him adapt to the fact that nighttime is for sleep, not interaction. This is another time when what feels right and loving is actually counter to what your child needs.

There is no right or wrong plan. What's most important is that you can enforce the limits you are setting. For example, telling a child to stay in his room is not a useful limit because you can't actually make him do that. If he can leave the room at will, he is in control. That is where a gate or door helper can be very useful. While it may feel uncomfortable to erect this boundary, it is much more loving than engaging in the ugly tug-of-war that tends to take place when children repeatedly come out of their rooms after bedtime.

It's all in the way you execute the plan. There's a big difference between taking a harsh and threatening approach and a loving and empathic one. Threatening "If you don't stay in your room, we will put up a gate to make you stay in there!" engages your child's negativity and defiance. This is the perfect setup for a protracted power struggle. Instead, explain calmly and matter-of-factly that "The rule at bedtime is you stay in your room so you can calm your mind and body to sleep. If you choose to come out, we will escort you back and put up our friend 'Mr. Gate,' who helps you stay in your room." It is important and helpful to acknowledge to your child that you fully understand that she may not like the new plan. That's okay—you don't expect her to. But you will still be setting this limit because it's your job as a parent to keep her healthy and safe. You are explaining the reasoning behind your plan, which is important. You are not justifying nor defending your plan. Most children know their parents dread the tantrum and will do anything to head it off. When you let your child know that it's okay if she doesn't like the rule and that you are not afraid of her melting down, it diffuses the power of the protest. This means being careful to refrain from trying to talk your child into accepting the limit as that communicates that the plan depends on her buy-in. It is the rare child who is going to respond with "That's a great idea, Mom and Dad. I know how important it is for me to get a good night's sleep, so I'm glad you will limit books and cuddle time and that you will put up a boundary to help me stay in my room."

Let your child know exactly what the plan will be. Children thrive when they know what to expect. Devise a plan that you feel is loving and appropriate and that you can follow through on, no matter how much pushback you get. Then, clearly lay it out for your child, step-by-step. If or when he protests any part of the plan, reiterate that you fully understand his perspective—that he doesn't like a three-book limit or that daddy isn't going to fall asleep next to him. And that's okay, you are not asking or expecting him to like it, but you will still be following through on it. Expect that it will get worse before it gets better. Many kids up the ante to see whether their parents are really going to stick to the limits. Once they see that you are not changing your mind, the coping and adaptation begin, as evidenced by the real-life stories shared in these pages.

FINAL THOUGHTS

Whatever plan you come up with, what's most important is that you are loving, clear, and consistent. When your child is losing it, he needs you to be his rock—to stay loving and present even in the face of his protests and, sometimes, vitriol. When the rules keep changing, it causes confusion: children don't know what to expect or where the boundaries are. They keep testing to see where the porous "gray" area is that they can exploit. Remember, children are strategic, not manipulative; they're trying to get you back into their room and avoid bedtime, not drive you crazy. So take the time you need to develop a plan that you feel you can implement. Play out all the possible scenarios, and be sure you feel ready to maintain the limit, no matter how hard your child protests. Otherwise, you are more likely to cave, and the cycle will continue.

While sleep challenges present some of the most difficult parenting moments, helping your child establish good sleep habits is the gift that keeps on giving. Not only does it improve your child's (and your) health and well-being, but you are also building her confidence that she can master the range of challenges she will face as she grows up.

6

POTTY LEARNING

Omar, almost four, is a feisty little guy who is fierce about asserting control over his world. He wants to do everything by himself, which has resulted in many a power struggle in the past eight months.

When Omar started to show interest in using the potty at around two and a quarter, his parents, Shawna and Philip, put a kids' potty in one of the bathrooms. Omar would sit on it from time to time, mostly fully dressed. He also asked to accompany his parents when they had to use the bathroom.

To build on this interest, Shawna and Philip started nudging Omar to use the potty. They offered all sorts of incentives, such as candy, extra screen time, and a new toy, but none resulted in much progress. As they continued to try to coax him, he started to proclaim that he would do it when he turned three. When that day came and went, he moved the needle to three and a half. Shawna and Philip were getting increasingly anxious about Omar's resistance to toilet training. They continued to try to coax him with rewards and then started to compare him to his schoolmates, who were all using the toilet at school. Still no progress.

When he was about three and three-quarters, they decided to do a "boot camp" (a strategy that entails taking diapers away and generally requires parents to play an active role in getting their child to use the toilet). Their close friends had successfully used this system with their three-year-old. For Omar, it was an "epic fail." Every time Shawna or Philip picked him up to put him on the toilet, when it looked like he needed to go, he screamed at the top of his lungs and ran off as soon as they placed him on the potty. When they repeatedly asked him if he needed to use the toilet, he would say "no"; then minutes later he would pee on the floor. He had repeated pee accidents and at one point withheld his bowel movements for three days. That's when they threw in the towel on bootcamp, but there was fallout. Omar became constipated from holding in his bowel movements. The doctor started him on MiraLAX to soften his stool and resolve the constipation, and referred Shawna and Philip to me.

At any given time, as many as half of the families I am working with are struggling with a potty learning challenge. Most of these children are three years old or older and have the ability to use the potty, meaning they have the physical capacity to control their bowel and bladder. There is an obstacle to mastering this skill that is emotional—an association has been made with the pottying process that is getting in the way of their moving forward to master this skill.

By the time families come to me for help, they have tried everything they can think of, including rewards and consequences, setting limits around using the potty (e.g., establishing times the child has to sit on the potty and try to go), shaming ("only babies go in diapers"), and threats (taking away desired items or activities). Nothing has worked.

As we peel back the layers to figure out why their children are resistant to using the toilet, several key insights emerge.

Parents are functioning from the faulty mindset that *it is their job to get their child trained*. The notion of having to "train" their child results in parents using a range of intrusive and forceful tactics to try to control their children and make them eliminate their pee and poop in the potty. This state of mind—that they can and need to control their children—is exacerbated by the fact that many of these parents from the get-go approached the whole potty learning process with a lot of anxiety. They had heard horror stories of catastrophic bootcamps, kids refusing to poop on the potty, and preschools rejecting children for not being trained. So, when they decided it was time to start "training" their own kids, they were already feeling tense, which set the tone for the process.

As counterintuitive as it may seem, parental overinvolvement and efforts to control their children are often a primary part of the problem when it comes to potty learning. For children, gaining control of their pee and poop is all about self-regulation, which they learn when you show that you believe in their ability to master this skill. (For this reason, I now refer to this process as "potty learning," instead of "potty training.") It just so happens that the age at which most children have the skills to learn to use the potty coincides with the developmental stage when children are becoming increasingly aware that they are separate beings and their body belongs only to them. This sense of ownership makes them even more sensitive to people trying to control their bodily functions (diapering, feeding, dressing, etc.). This desire for control extends beyond their bodies to the whole world. "By myself!" and "I do it!" are frequent refrains. Accordingly, some amount of defiance and opposition is developmentally appropriate and expected at this stage and is often triggered by others' attempts to control them.

It is also important to keep the temperament factor in mind: children who, by nature, tend to be more controlling and have a harder time being flexible and adapting to change are especially sensitive and reactive to feeling controlled. When it comes to potty learning, this means that the more you try to control your child's elimination, the more likely she is to dig in her heels and resist. This is how your child maintains her integrity and reminds you that she is the only one who has the power to control her body.

You can see, then, how the typical tactics many parents employ to motivate their child to use the potty not only backfire but often amplify and perpetuate the challenge their child is experiencing. All the rewarding, bribery, and threats of negative consequences end up complicating and thwarting the process, making it less likely their child will master this new skill.

Parents are approaching the potty process through their adult, logical lens. "Wouldn't you prefer to pee and poop on the potty when it is so much simpler, less messy, and less time consuming than going in a diaper or pull-up?" "Don't you want to be a big boy like your friends?" The problem is that children who have the physical ability to eliminate on the toilet but are not doing so are driven not by rationality but by emotional associations with and meaning they have made of this process. Thus, using logic with them is not helpful.

For example, some children associate using the potty with a fear that this step toward independence may mean that mommy and daddy won't pay as much attention to and care for them in the same way—that there will be some loss of love. This is often the case when there is a new baby in the home. The older child sees all the attention being paid to her younger sibling and wants to be a baby again, too. That is why older children who had mastered potty learning before the birth of the new baby often regress in this process. Trying to coax these kids to use the potty by reminding them that they are "big kids" backfires because they have no interest in being big; they are, in fact, aiming to be little again.

Children who are highly sensitive to their bodily experiences sometimes develop fears about part of themselves disappearing down a drain. These are the kids who freak out when they accidentally pee or poop on the potty. (They are sitting on the potty either because their parent has required them to do so or they just meant to explore/pretend and they unintentionally pee or poop.) The experience of this sudden loss of control over their bodies triggers them into panic mode and can result in more fervent resistance to using the potty.

When it comes to challenges in the potty learning process, it is important to keep in mind that children are not a monolithic group. They have different temperaments, developmental paths, and life experiences that affect all aspects of their functioning, including learning to use the potty. There is no one-size-fits-all approach that works for every child and family. When I collaborate with parents to address these challenges, we look at all the factors that might be influencing the process. We root out the underlying causes to come up with a solution for their unique child—to get him unstuck, so to speak.

Here is how the process worked for Omar, Maddie, and Isaiah. Note that, unlike the other chapters in this book, I am not going to go through all the mindsets and mindshifts for each case because they are all the same. The faulty mindset is parents feeling they can and need to control their child—to *make* him use the potty. The mindshift is that *only their child controls his pee or poop. The more parents try to force the process, the less likely it is that their child will learn to master this skill.* Through these stories, I show how pulling back from their need to control the pottying process enables parents to tune in to the root cause of the obstacle to their child's success and to implement a plan that sets their child up for success.

OMAR: BOOTCAMP DEBACLE

The Assessment

Trying to control Omar is backfiring. The rewards/bribes are failing because they are experienced by Omar as an effort to control him at a time when his number one goal is to be the boss of everything. The bootcamp failed for the same reason. Telling him he had no other choice but to use the potty, and then picking him up in the middle of peeing or pooping, only fueled his need to show Shawna and Philip that no one controls his body but him. This led to his withholding his bowel movements, something he had never previously done.

Coaxing him to act his age and comparing him to his classmates is not having the desired effect. It is making Omar feel ashamed, which is more paralyzing than motivating.

Omar's pronouncement that he will start to use the potty sometime down the road is a tactic to get his parents off of his case. Their agenda is loud and clear. He knows how much they want him to use the potty. Assuring them that it will happen at some point in the future serves to reduce the pressure he is feeling. It may certainly also be aspirational. (I find that most kids want to use the potty. They are just stuck—the situation has taken on a life of its own and is fraught with tension. The anxiety is paralyzing to kids.)

To help Omar take positive steps in the pottying process, first, the constipation needs to be resolved so that Omar no longer associates bowel movements with discomfort.

The Plan

Shawna and Philip dial it all back. We agree that the first step needs to be communicating to Omar that he is in total control of his pee and poop and that mommy and daddy will no longer be trying to make him go. "Mommy and Daddy have been so silly! We have been trying to get you to use the potty because that's what we do. It's what feels good to us. We don't have to get all cleaned up, and it takes less time than diapers. So we figured it would be better for you, too. But that was so silly because only you know what your body needs. Your body, your choice. It's your job to take care of it. (Kids love the idea of having a job.

It's empowering.) So, when it comes to peeing and pooping, you are the decider about where you let it go, either in a diaper/pull-up or the toilet. From now on, it's all up to you. It doesn't matter to us as long as you let the pee and poop out. It's not healthy for it to stay stuck in your body." This discussion is purposefully designed to be lighthearted—to ease the tension that is usually pervasive around pottying at this point in the process. It is a total one-eighty.

They also show Omar a video designed to help kids understand how poop works and why it is so important to let it go, for health reasons. (See the appendix for information on how to access the video.)

They are clear about Omar's choices and show confidence in his ability to make the best decisions for himself. "What's so awesome is that you've got two great choices: since you know how to hold your pee and poop in until you want to let it go, one choice is to use the toilet. If you make that choice, you can wear underwear. If you choose not to use the potty, you will wear a pull-up, which will be changed when it is full of pee or poop because it's not healthy for your body to sit in a soiled pull-up. Having pee or poop on your skin causes rashes." (It is critical that the rules be presented matter-of-factly, without any suggestion that one choice is preferable over another. The second your child picks up on your preference, it becomes fodder for resistance. The idea is to make this a matter-of-fact, rather than emotionally charged, process.)

They go through the natural consequences of using diapers versus going on the potty. They tell Omar that, when he chooses to use the potty, he will be able to stay in the pool longer because the swim diaper gets full quickly. They also point out that, in general, he will have more time to play because using the potty takes less time than changing a diaper. (Sometimes, parents use role-playing. They time how long it takes to do a diaper/pull-up change versus how long it takes to use the potty. For the latter, parents ask their child if he wants to be timed to see how long it takes to use the potty or if he wants to time mom or dad. On several occasions, kids who have been refusing to use the toilet go ahead and sit on it as part of the experiment and end up actually peeing or pooping in the potty, which gets them over the hump and on their way. Regardless, kids generally find this whole experiment very amusing, and it can be the linchpin for some.)

Shawna and Philip also explain that Omar can stay for lunch bunch at preschool, which requires kids to use the potty. They are very careful not to use a tone that conveys they are trying to convince him to use the potty, as he would pick up on that in a heartbeat. They lay this information out as facts for him to consider as he makes his choice.

They follow Omar's lead; they stop talking about the potty unless Omar brings it up. Shawna and Philip see how constantly talking about the potty—asking if he has to go, suggesting they read books on the topic—is messaging to Omar how desperate they are for him to use the toilet. (Kids are very astute; they tune right into your agenda, and their instinct to resist kicks in.) Shawna and Philip read books about going to the potty only when Omar requests them. They ask him if he has to go to the bathroom only at natural junctures in the day—at bedtime, at morning wake up, and before getting into the car. If he says he doesn't have to go, they move on. They do not cross the line by trying to coax him to change his mind, which would send the message that they know his body better than he does.

They engage his lovey (Pringle the Pig) in the process. During pretend play, Shawna and Philip occasionally start to integrate the idea that Pringle has to pee, and they wonder whether Omar can help him. The idea is to put Omar in the role of "teacher" while also giving him practice with the process through the safety of pretend play.

The Outcome

The first few days of enacting the new plan, nothing changes, but then Omar starts to ask his parents whether he can have extra TV time if he uses the potty. As hard as this is for Shawna and Philip, they respond: "Omar, we are not giving rewards for using the potty. That is something you either choose to do or not to do. The reward is that you feel good about taking care of your body and you get to go to lunch bunch. It is your decision." His retort: "I don't care about lunch bunch" (which they know isn't true but wisely refrain from challenging).

After staying this course and being completely nonreactive, within two weeks, Omar starts to pee on the potty. Shawna and Philip resist the powerful impulse to celebrate and instead focus on *his* accomplishment: "You felt the pee had to come and got yourself to the potty. You did a great job of taking care of yourself. Now, you have more time to play." This is another one of those counterintuitive phenomena; when you smother your child with praise, you are communicating that his action/choice made *you* happy. This makes potty learning a relationship issue, something that has the power to please or disappoint you. The pressure they experience confounds the process for children and causes anxiety, which interferes in their ability to make progress. You want *your child to own his achievement*, to experience the intrinsic reward of becoming more self-sufficient.

Within a month, Omar is peeing and pooping on the potty regularly. When he has the occasional accident, Shawna and Philip deal with it very straightforwardly: "No problem. Let's get you cleaned up. Would you like to put on a pull-up or underwear?" They continue to provide these choices even as Omar starts to use the potty more frequently to emphasize that they have no preference. A family I worked with many years ago had implemented a very similar plan to this one. Their daughter had started to choose underwear and use the toilet consistently for five days in a row. On the sixth day, when they opened the undies drawer, she chose a pull-up. Impulsively, they responded, "But, sweetie, you have been doing such a great job using the potty. Don't you want to wear underwear?" This resulted in a weeklong backslide. Once they got back on the bandwagon, not suggesting in any way, shape, or form that they were invested in her using the toilet, their daughter made great progress and became fully potty independent.

MADDIE: POTTY REGRESSION

Maddie, age four, had been completely potty trained for almost a year. Then COVID-19 hit, and, by the second month of lockdown, she starts to have pee accidents. Her parents, Mitchell and Sarah, are vexed by this. Life is stressful enough. They become increasingly frustrated and punitive with her. They try taking away toys and screen time. They express anger about the fact that she knows how to use the potty and is purposefully making messes. They ask her what her friends and teachers would think if they saw her acting like a baby. None of these tactics work. So they resort to instituting specific times Maddie has to sit on the potty. She complies, but most of the time she doesn't pee or poop. Often, minutes later, she has an accident. Mitchell and Sarah are at their wits' end and worried about what this means for Maddie when she returns to school.

The Assessment

Maddie is not having accidents on purpose. Maddie is a highly sensitive child who has a hard time with transitions. She likes predictability—to know exactly what to expect. She is the kid who at preschool points out to the teacher a mix-up in the schedule or when another child's placemat is in the wrong space on the table. She melts down if dad comes to get her in the morning when she wakes up instead of mom, whom she was expecting. The changes that have taken place in her world due to the coronavirus have been especially challenging for her. In addition to the potty regression, Maddie's frustration tolerance is much lower and she is having more tantrums. She is also demanding that her mom lie down with her until she falls asleep at night, something Sarah has not done for years.

Taking a punitive, shaming approach is unlikely to help Maddie regain her previous, higher level of functioning. It is likely to increase her anxiety, which will hurt her ability to act more competently and independently. Maddie needs support, not shame.

Trying to force Maddie to go by making her sit on the potty is backfiring. The core struggle for Maddie in this moment is feeling out of control given that her world has turned upside down. The more Mitchell and Sarah try to control her, the more Maddie digs in her heels to regain some sense of agency and control over her world.

The Plan

Mitchell and Sarah validate and show a lot of empathy for how the lockdown has changed their worlds and how hard that is for Maddie. They empathize with how much she misses her teachers and friends, and that it can be frustrating when mommy and daddy have to work so much and can't play all the time. They know that dealing with these changes has made it harder for her to have the energy to practice skills, such as sleeping on her own and going to the potty.

They tell Maddie that they believe in her and know that, when she's ready, she will use the potty again. They emphasize that she knows her body best and is the only one in control of it.

They do a complete one-eighty. They stop engaging in any strategies to get Maddie to use the toilet.

When Maddie has an accident, they approach it very matter-of-factly. They do not shame. They simply help her get cleaned up and move on, without saying a word about it.

They set a reasonable limit on underwear use. If she has more than three accidents a day, it will be time to change into a pull-up. They are very careful to communicate this dispassionately, to make clear that underwear is not a reward and pull-ups are not a punishment. They simply explain that underwear is not made for pee and poop. If she is not going on the potty, then the option is pull-ups. They emphasize that a pull-up is great because it can hold the pee and poop. But, if she decides she wants to use the potty, she can always just pull it down like underwear and go. (The idea is to message that she has lots of choices while also setting objective, reasonable limits. Most parents find it hard to tolerate repeated accidents all day long.)

The Outcome

The first day of the new plan, when Maddie has a third accident by noon, Mitchell and Sarah let her know it's time for a pull-up. While Maddie had shown acceptance of the plan that they had laid out, in real time she strongly rejects the idea of going back into a pull-up during the day. (She still wears one at night.) Mitchell and Sarah calmly remind Maddie that the rule is if underwear is soiled three times, she goes into a pull-up. But seeing that the idea of the pull-up is such a disincentive for Maddie, they spontaneously decide to offer another choice: if Maddie decides to use the potty the next two times she has to go, she can go back into underwear. (Remember, this is not a reward but a natural consequence; wearing underwear is the logical outcome of choosing to use the potty.) That did it. Her desire to stay in underwear is the ticket. She uses the potty for the rest of the day for pee and continues to pee exclusively in the potty.

Pooping on the potty takes longer. While Maddie is regularly wearing underwear all day at this point, every night, right before bed, she asks for her diaper and immediately makes a bowel movement. (It is amazing how children's bodies regulate to eliminate at times they are most comfortable, often first thing in the morning or right when they return from childcare or school.) Mitchell and Sarah are anxious about this pattern. But experience has taught them that taking any kind of coaxing or coercive approach backfires. They stay the course, not saying a word about her poop. Three weeks into the new plan, one night while in the bath, Maddie jumps out, sits herself on the potty and poops. She shouts with elation, "I did it! Mommy, see my poop in the potty?" Mitchell and Sarah acknowledge how pleased she is with herself. They are very careful not to throw a potty party or to make the focus how proud they are of her to avoid making this accomplishment about pleasing them. Within a week of this first potty poop, Maddie is using the toilet for bowel movements consistently. Of note is that Mitchell and Sarah also start to see a more global change in Maddie. She is having fewer meltdowns over minor issues and is more resilient overall. Taking back control of her body seems to have had a more pervasive, positive impact.

ISAIAH: PETER PAN SYNDROME

Isaiah is almost age three and three-quarters. His parents, Mariah and Bruce, started talking about and coaxing him to use the potty when he turned three. They tried rewards and bribery, comparing him to his friends, and trying to convince him how much easier it will be to use the potty. His response has been consistent; he says he is scared of the potty. However, while he has never used the toilet at home, his teacher reports that he consistently uses it at school to pee. Isaiah is also still in a crib and refuses to use a "big boy" cup. He prefers to drink from a sippy cup lying down on his back, often asking to lean against a parent as he guzzles. Isaiah also whines a lot and acts very helpless, always wanting his mom or his older sister (who loves to be his caretaker) to do things for him that he is capable of doing for himself.

The Assessment

The tactics Mariah and Bruce are using to try to convince Isaiah to get interested in using the toilet are backfiring. This is because they are not addressing the underlying cause: that Isaiah does not see himself as a big boy who is capable of caring for himself. He has not shown the natural motivation to do things independently that is typical of children his age. He is triggered to feel helpless the second he faces any kind of challenge, even something as seemingly minor as choosing which superhero action figure he wants in his crib at bedtime. He gets himself into a total tizzy trying to make a decision and eventually demands that mom choose. He wants his parents, especially Mariah, to do everything for him—behavior consistent with a much younger child. We agree that Isaiah's self-narrative is an important piece of the puzzle that explains why he lacks any interest in taking responsibility for his elimination. Part of the overall strategy needs to include helping Isaiah see himself as a competent kid who has the ability to do more for himself.

The Plan

Before addressing potty learning, Mariah and Bruce focus on building Isaiah's confidence. They start with addressing Isaiah's helplessness. When he whines, they lovingly tell him that they will be happy to help him when he can use a voice they can understand. (They refrain from calling this his "big boy" voice because that can come off as shaming. We are also concerned that Isaiah might not be so invested in being a big boy right now.)

When he complains he can't do something on his own that he is perfectly capable of, they let him know they will help him think through how to accomplish the task but will not do it for him. If he gets frustrated by this response, they calmly let him know that when he's ready to try, they can't wait to work with him to find a solution.

Within a few days of executing this new approach, they can already see a difference. Isaiah is whining less and showing more fortitude in sticking with challenging tasks and activities.

They move all elimination-related tasks to the bathroom. Up until this time, Mariah and Bruce have been changing Isaiah while he is lying down on the floor, as if he were a much younger child. They explain to him that the new plan is that all pee and poop tasks happen in the bathroom, whether or not he is using the potty, because that is the appropriate venue. They change him standing up and give him some jobs to help, like learning to wipe himself and throwing away the soiled diaper so he is more involved in self-care.

They do away with the sippy cup. Mariah and Bruce tell Isaiah that they are in big trouble with Dr. O'Brien, his pediatrician. They explain that, when they told her that they were still giving Isaiah a sippy cup, she exclaimed, "'What? Isaiah? Are you kidding? That guy? He is totally ready for an open cup. Mom and Dad, parents aren't supposed to give kids sippy cups once they turn three. And Isaiah should be sitting up while drinking! Lying down is not healthy.' Oh boy, mommy and daddy have been making big mistakes!" (Isaiah finds this hilarious. He cracks up as Mariah does this dramatic retelling of their conversation with his beloved pediatrician.)

Mariah and Bruce explain that the new plan is that all beverages will go in the open cup and Isaiah needs to be sitting up to drink. They give him a choice of many different colored straws, to give him some sense of control over this big change, which he loves. He adapts to this new expectation immediately. Mariah and Bruce begin to see that Isaiah was primed for this leap forward in his development and that they had been enabling him by maintaining such low expectations of him. The proof is when his older sister, age seven, is helping to cut vegetables using a knife. Isaiah asks to do the same. Mariah's knee-jerk response is, "No, knives are not for three-year-olds." Isaiah retorts: "I can do it!" Stunned, Mariah locates a safe plastic knife he can use. He is elated to be a kitchen helper.

They apply this new approach to bedtime. They successfully set limits that lead to Isaiah learning to feel safe and secure falling asleep without Mariah sitting next to his crib rubbing his back. They start by trying to take a gradual approach that entails Mariah staying in the room and moving farther away from the crib each night, but that only results in Isaiah constantly trying to engage Mariah and get her to move closer, rather than focusing on falling asleep. When they change the plan to Mariah leaving and doing one check with a mantra, Isaiah protests hard the first two nights, but he adapts and is sleeping independently by the third night.

Mariah and Bruce are able to implement this loving and effective new plan because they no longer fear the tantrums that still sometimes happen when they don't give Isaiah what he wants. They know that the tantrum in itself is not harmful to Isaiah and that giving in is enabling. Setting these higher expectations is what will help him develop the coping skills he needs to feel more confident and be more resilient. (As for Isaiah still being in a crib at almost four years old, while we agree that it would be better for him from a maturity and social–emotional perspective to sleep in a toddler bed, we decide that it would be best to hold off on another big change until after tackling the potty issue.)

With Isaiah feeling more competent, Mariah and Bruce decide it's the right time to set a higher expectation for his ability to use the potty. They are confident he is able to do it because he uses the potty at school more often than not. They start by telling him "You are not going to believe it, but we are in trouble again with the doctor!" (Having responded so well to this approach with regard to the sippy cup, they have decided to employ it again.) They continue: "When we told Dr. O'Brien that you were still using diapers, she was like, 'What? Isaiah, the guy who can do so many things for himself? Mom and Dad, you are making a big mistake! When kids turn three, they are totally able to use the potty. And Isaiah? He's totally got this. He'll show you.'" Mariah concludes with "Can you believe mommy and daddy messed up again? So Friday (it was Wednesday) will be the last day for diapers. Just like you figured out how to use the open cup instead of the sippy cup, we know you'll figure out how to use the potty when you're ready." Interestingly and surprising to them, Isaiah responds: "I know how to use the potty. I just don't *want* to use it." They respond: "Well, that's totally up to you, isn't it?" They are very careful to keep messaging that they are not trying to make him do anything. They are just setting the limit of no more diapers and that it's his job to decide what to do with his pee and poop. The idea is that he will decide on his own that it's better to use the potty than to keep having accidents.

That is the whole plan. It is predicated on the idea that, for Isaiah, less intervention is more. Isaiah has already shown that, once the expectations are raised and Mariah and Bruce take a matter-of-fact "this is what is happening now because you are so capable" approach, Isaiah quickly rises to the occasion. They have learned that Isaiah thrives when the plan is totally clear, as they learned with both the sippy cup and sleep interventions.

While this may sound like bootcamp, this approach is quite different. Most bootcamps are adult driven and involve a range of tactics to coax the child to use the toilet: constant reminders about using the potty, requirements for sitting on the potty at certain times of day for set periods of time, picking children up in the middle of peeing or pooping and placing them on the toilet, and providing rewards for using the potty. These are all very intrusive measures. The approach Mariah and Bruce take is guided by completely different principles. There is no adult intervention, except to provide whatever help Isaiah asks for, and there is no pressure applied. Potty learning entails trusting the child to figure out how to control his body in an age-appropriate way and to master a new ability that he already has the skills to achieve.

The Outcome

The first day of the new plan, Isaiah repeatedly asks for a pull-up. Mariah and Bruce calmly remind him that there are no more pull-ups during the day. They reiterate that they are confident he will figure out where it is best for him to let his pee and poop go.

He has accidents the entire first day. Mariah and Bruce deal with them matter-of-factly. They decide to arrange a "cleanup station" in the bathroom with underwear, pants, and wipes in the bathroom. They explain to Isaiah that, because he is so good at taking care of his body, it is his job to help get himself cleaned up. (The idea is to keep messaging that they believe in his ability to take good care of himself and that they are not upset by his accidents. It is all up to him. They are confident that the discomfort of having repeated accidents will be the motivator for Isaiah to make a different choice.)

On the second day, we add a little reverse psychology to the plan. Recalling Isaiah's assertion that he already knows perfectly well how to use the potty, we decide that when he has an accident, Mariah and Bruce will make a point of saying, "No worries; looks like you're just not ready to use the potty" (which they communicate matter-of-factly, without any judgment). It works like a charm. Isaiah is so motivated to prove them wrong that he marches right to the bathroom and pees on the potty. Mariah and Bruce respond: "Well, I guess we were wrong! Mommy and daddy keep making mistakes. Dr. O'Brien was right! We'll have to let her know."

Isaiah has a few accidents over the course of the next few days, but by day five he is mostly accident free. Further, mastering another major milestone results in continued progress in Isaiah's growing confidence to do things more independently. There are fewer battles to get through daily tasks, such as getting dressed in the morning. And his disposition is much more positive overall.

OTHER TYPICAL CHALLENGES THAT ARISE IN THE POTTY LEARNING PROCESS

Constipation. By the time families come to see me about a potty learning challenge, many of their children are holding in their bowel movements. This is most often the case when parents have been trying to control the potty process. The constipation results in hard stools, which makes pooping painful and adds another layer of stress to the process.

If your child is constipated, explain to him very matter-of-factly that letting go of his poop is very important for his health. Holding it in makes the poop hard and painful to push out. There is a video you can find in the appendix that can be helpful to view with your child. It illustrates why and how we poop and what happens when we hold it in. (Be sure to view it in advance. You know your child best and can assess whether you think it will be useful for him.) Taking a scientific approach can be very effective for helping children see that *they are making choices about how to eliminate* and that each choice has an outcome.

If your child is constipated, it is important to talk to his health care provider, who may prescribe a stool softener. As long as your child's bowel movements are hard, it is unlikely he will feel comfortable letting go. Be sure to work with your provider on establishing a dose that softens your child's bowel movements but doesn't make them so loose that your child can't control them. This can intensify the problem. Remember, it's all about control.

Children wearing underwear but then asking for a diaper or pull-up to poop. This is very frustrating and confounding for parents. Your child clearly has all the skills she needs to use the potty. She is able to hold her pee and poop and then let it go when she chooses. She's just doing it in a diaper versus the toilet. *She is almost there.* Avoid the temptation, at this juncture, to try to coax, cajole, or get your child to cross the finish line, as these tactics often set kids back. Instead, reinforce the idea that it is your child's choice while setting appropriate boundaries around toileting.

You can tell your child that when kids are three years old (or whatever age you decide), pee and poop are done in the bathroom, whether they are using a pull-up or the potty. By this time, most children have observed many peers using the potty and they see their parents going into the bathroom all the time. So this will make sense to them.

There is an expectation that she will participate in the process. This conveys that she is capable of doing a lot of her own self-care and you are supporting that. If your child is still in diapers, switch to pull-ups because she can put them on herself when she needs to poop. You can place a pile of pull-ups in the bathroom and have her take responsibility for the whole process, if she is physically capable of doing this. She can take her underwear off, put the pull-up on, and do her business. Then, you help her take it off and put the poop in the toilet, wash her hands, and get herself dressed again.

It is by experiencing the outcome of their choices that children learn to make good decisions. The goal is for her to eventually see that it's more beneficial *to her* to go on the potty than have to keep changing pull-ups; but she can only make this objective assessment if she is not reacting to feeling pushed or pressured.

Children who actively resist or say they are afraid of using the potty. There are a range of reasons this may happen. The most common ones I see are:

- **A sensory-based issue.** Children who are underresponsive to bodily sensations may not be bothered by a full diaper and may be less tuned in to the signs of having to pee and poop. Others are oversensitive to sensory input. For example, some children are overwhelmed by the loud flushing sound, especially the automatic ones in public bathrooms. Some children with tactile sensitivity may not like the feel of pee splashing up onto them or of poop coming out. And smells, like those common in bathrooms, can be overwhelming. These are experiences that children are often not conscious of and can't articulate. What they can express to you is that they are afraid of using the potty. If you think the cause of the delay in or resistance to potty learning may be in part due to your child's sensory experience of the process, explore ways to reduce the sensory discomfort. For example, if the flushing sound is the issue, you do the flushing after she's done. One family had their child wear headphones, especially when she went into public restrooms where the noise level is hard to control. If the problem persists despite these kinds of accommodations, I recommend you consult with an occupational therapist (OT). OTs are highly skilled at helping children process sensory input accurately so they can master new skills more readily.

- **Feeling unstable on toilets that are too high to enable their feet to be firmly planted.** Be sure to have a "squatty potty," a footstool that fits around the base of the toilet where your child can securely rest his feet.

- **A major change in your child's world, such as a new baby, a recent loss, a family move, or a change in child-care arrangements.** If this is the case, I recommend giving your child time to adapt and get back to his baseline of feeling secure in his world before working on a new skill. Keep in mind that if the change is a new baby in the family, your child may be much less interested in being a "big boy." He sees the baby getting so much attention for being dependent, including being diapered. Using the "you're a big boy" tactic to try to coax your child to use the toilet can also be interpreted as shaming. Remember, shame is paralyzing, not motivating. It can negatively affect a child's self-esteem and thwart her ability to tackle new challenges.

Children who are showing no interest in using the potty. Following are strategies I have found effective in helping children who by age two and a half to three move forward—the age by which most children are taking steps in the pottying process.

- **Use pretend play to give your child a chance to practice and get comfortable with the process.** You might build into the story you are creating together the idea that your child's lovey (or action figure, doll, animal, etc.) needs to learn to use the potty so he can swim in the big kid pool or go to the camp he wants to attend. Through the play, encourage your child to be a helper. Have your child take the pretend toy through all the steps of going to the potty. If you have a sense of what the obstacle might be for your child, for example, being afraid of the unknown or feeling pressure to perform, work that into the play. Have your child be the one who helps his lovey get over the fear. This can be very empowering to children, especially those who have expressed fear about using the potty. It helps them work through whatever anxieties they may have about the process.
- **See whether your child wants to sit on the potty with his pull-ups on.** Then, make an activity out of cutting holes in the pull-ups, which your child then wears to sit on the potty and eliminate. Once he gets comfortable making his pee and poop this way, he may eventually forgo the pull-up altogether.
- **Ask your child if she wants to practice using the potty.** You tell her that you know that she isn't feeling ready to use the potty yet, but, if she wants, she can practice. Remind her of other times she has been fearful of or resistant to trying something new, but with practice was able to master the challenge. The idea of practicing takes pressure off and can sometimes be the key to kids feeling more comfortable taking the next step in the process. (If your child hedges, back off. Remember, once your child says no, it's important not to cross the line into convincing or cajoling to push your agenda.) Go through all the steps. Let her choose a pair of underwear, have her pretend she feels some pee coming, provide whatever help she needs to pull her pants down or lift her skirt or dress up, and then have her choose which potty to sit on and pretend to let the pee and poop out. Having a chance to practice through pretend can ease anxiety and make children more comfortable with the process. Using the pull-up with the hole in it can also be used for practicing.

- **Set a specific date for when there will be no more diapers and pull-ups (for children three and older).** This is the plan we implemented for Isaiah. You matter-of-factly explain that there will be no more diapers on a date in the very near future. (You don't want to tell them more than a few days in advance. That can cause anxiety as they anticipate the change.) *But you don't say anything about having to use the toilet.* While this sounds odd, telling her she *has* to use it may trigger defiance and make it less likely she will use the potty. You simply explain, "There are no more diapers during the day when kids turn three and a half, so starting Friday, it's underwear during the day and pull-ups at night." If your child protests, you fully acknowledge her feelings: "I know this is a big change and that you may not agree with it or like it, but that is the plan. We have total confidence that you'll figure it out."

  Point out other changes your child has faced and mastered, such as having to give up the bottle and pacifier even when she didn't feel ready, to remind her that she is capable of adapting to changes. Emphasize that she is still in complete control of her body. You are not making her do anything. If she goes on the potty, fine. If she has an accident, no problem; you will clean it up together and move on. This initially feels uncomfortable to parents. But, remember, when children sense their parents have an agenda or expectations, it causes anxiety and pressure that interferes in learning. Accidents are part of the process. They should not result in shaming or annoyance. Once children experience that it is all up to them—they don't have anything to rebel against—they are more likely to make the best decision for themselves, which is to use the potty. Few children would prefer to have accidents all day long that they are responsible for helping to clean up.

  If your child still needs to wear a diaper at naptime and overnight, state matter-of-factly that the rule is diapers are only used at those times. One family had their child fill one box with diapers to use for sleep times and another to give away to children who are under three who still use diapers during the day. Just the act of being involved in the plan can give your child a sense of control.

While this may sound similar to a bootcamp, it is, in fact, quite different. As I mentioned earlier, most bootcamps are adult driven and designed to control your child. They involve intrusive tactics, such as requiring children to sit on the potty for periods of time and transporting children in the middle of peeing or pooping to the potty. The approach I suggest doesn't tell the child what to do; it is all left in the child's hands. It is based on the concept that, when you trust your child to figure out how to control his body and don't push your agenda to try to control him, he is freed to overcome the obstacles that lead to mastery.

GUIDING PRINCIPLES FOR MAKING THE POTTY PROCESS POSITIVE, NOT PERILOUS

Learning to manage bodily functions, such as elimination, eating, and sleeping, is essential for children's sense of agency and self-esteem. It builds their confidence that they can be in control of and take care of themselves.

Be sure your child is ready. Signs that children are ready, which emerge roughly between 18 months and two and a half years, include the following:

- Staying dry for at least a two-hour period
- Recognizing that they are urinating or having a bowel movement
- Being able to follow simple instructions
- Wanting to come in the bathroom with you to watch how you use the potty
- Feeling uncomfortable in a soiled diaper and asking to be changed
- Wanting to sit on the potty, even if they don't pee or poop in it yet

If you push the process before your child is showing interest, he may sense that you are promoting your agenda. This can lead to that knee-jerk defiance that results when children feel you are trying to control them, thus turning the pottying process into a power struggle.

Explain to your child that it is her body and only she controls it, including choosing how to pee and poop. Point out all the positive ways she already controls her body, such as eating healthy foods to grow big and strong; getting herself to sleep to build her brain and body; or running, jumping, and climbing, which help her have fun on the playground equipment. The idea is to instill a sense of confidence in your child that she knows her own body and is capable of taking good care of herself.

She is the decider as to when she needs to go and whether to use the potty or a diaper or pull-up each day. *Remember, your job is to support your child in the process, not to control the process.* I suggest creating a drawer that has pull-ups or diapers on one side and underwear on the other. Each morning when your child gets dressed, you let her know that she gets to choose which she wears, reminding her that if she picks underwear it means she's deciding to use the potty. The more children feel that they are in control, the more likely it is that the process will go smoothly. I have seen even seemingly benign efforts to steer children backfire. (Recall the story above about the child who backslid big time when her parents crossed the line and urged her to choose underwear when she had picked a pull-up. The need to feel in control often supersedes everything!)

Provide whatever tools and support your child needs to feel comfortable using the potty. This might mean helping your child with getting his clothes off and on, wiping, and washing hands. As for which potty to use, let your child choose which one is most comfortable for him. Some children prefer using the adult toilet with an insert, while others like the kiddie potties. Giving children choices like this can be helpful because it gives them a sense of control. Be sure that whatever option your child uses enables him to have his feet firmly grounded. If he likes using a traditional, adult toilet, remember to have a squatty potty that fits around the base of the toilet where your child can rest his feet. This provides the physical sense of security and stability he needs to make the experience comfortable.

Take a scientific approach. Explain why we all pee and poop by saying that our body takes in what it needs from what we drink and eat and what our bodies don't need comes out as pee and poop. Then explain that people who use the potty wear underpants and people who choose not to use the potty wear diapers or pull-ups. To demonstrate, do a little experiment with your child. Take a pitcher of water and a wet ball of clay. Point out how the water has the consistency of pee, and the wet clay is like poop. Then pour water from the pitcher onto the underwear and then onto the diaper or pull-up to show how the water soaks through the underwear but not the diaper or pull-up. Do the same with the wet clay, which is absorbed by the diaper or pull-up but not the underwear. Make it very clear that it's their body and they get to choose which way they are going to let the pee and poop out. I find that when you take a teaching approach and emphasize that it's up to your child to decide how she will eliminate, she is freed to act on her drive for independence and master the skill, unimpeded by the pressure or anxiety she might experience when she knows the adults in her world want her "trained."

Pull-ups can be framed as a tool that gives your child choices and becomes part of the learning process. Help her practice putting the pull-up on and then pulling it down to show her that she can use it like underwear when she wants to use the potty. If she chooses not to use the potty, then she can pee and poop in it. No problem, it's her choice.

Focus on *your child's* accomplishments around potty use (not on how it affects you). Acknowledge her interest and the steps she is taking in the pottying process. Instead of saying things like "Mommy is so proud of you! You peed in the potty!" respond with something more like "You felt the pee had to come out and you got yourself to the bathroom and let it go in the potty. You took great care of your body. And no need to change a diaper, so you can get right back to playing." This keeps the focus on how using the potty benefits your child (not you) by acknowledging the steps *she* took to master this process. It's her victory.

When you have a big reaction about how excited and proud you are or, conversely, show disappointment (which is palpable to kids through your tone and body language, even when you don't say anything), it makes pottying a relationship issue. It is one of those counterintuitive aspects of parenting. We function from a place of logic. If we praise our children, they will want to do more of whatever it is that makes us happy and do less of things that disappoint us or make us angry. The problem is that, when your child's actions have the power to please or disappoint you, the process becomes emotional and personal and can put a lot of pressure on a child. This can interfere in, not support, the potty learning process.

Also note that, for some children who tend to be more sensitive by nature, a big parental reaction can be especially overwhelming and shut them down. Many families I work with report that when they exude a lot of excitement about their child having eliminated in the potty, their child bursts into tears and reverts to refusing to use the toilet.

Expect and handle potty accidents matter-of-factly, without anger, shaming, or punishment. Accidents are part of the process and should be handled dispassionately: "No problem, accidents happen. Let's get you cleaned up." Encourage your child to help in the process to support his learning to take responsibility for his body. He might be in charge of wiping up pee and then choosing a new pair of underwear. When you have a big reaction to accidents and show anger or disappointment (not just with words but with gestures, facial expressions, and heavy sighs), it makes children feel ashamed. This tends to increase accidents. It makes the whole elimination process anxiety producing, which interferes in your child's ability to master it.

If your child resists his diaper being changed or cleaning up after an accident, let him know that this isn't a choice. It is a health and safety issue. Having pee or poop stay next to his skin causes irritation and rashes, so it is your job to make sure he is changed right away, even if he doesn't like that plan. You then do it as quickly and dispassionately as possible and move on.

Let your child experience the natural consequences of her choices. For example, you are heading to the playground. You ask your child whether she has to use the potty. She says she doesn't have to go. You resist coaxing, cajoling, or bribing and instead explain, "It's your body, so you know best what you need. If you have to go when we are at the playground we will just need to go home." This is not punishment and is never said as a threat. It is a matter-of-fact outcome of her choice. If your child has an accident, you take her home as part of the plan you have established. Then, the next time you are leaving the house, you can remind her of her choices. Children learn from experience. If peeing or pooping in their clothes means needing to leave the playground early, they are likely to decide on their own to use the potty before their next trip to the park.

WHAT TO AVOID

There are a number of pitfalls parents fall into when it comes to potty learning that can interfere with, rather than support, the process.

Introducing potty learning when a big change is on the horizon or has just taken place. Any significant change in a child's world can make him feel out of control, such as an upcoming or recent family move, a new childcare arrangement, or welcoming a new baby into the family. Children don't have the perspective required to make sense of what these changes mean, which leads to feeling unstable and insecure until, with time, they see that all is still right with the world. Since learning to use the potty is all about control, it is best not to focus on or expect your child to master this skill at a time when he is coping with another significant change in his life.

Forcing. You are on risky ground anytime you cross the line from providing support to trying to control your child. One common scenario is telling a child she has to sit on the potty after she's said she doesn't have to go. This communicates that you know her body better than she does, which interferes with her ability to self-regulate. This tactic can also be experienced as intrusive for many children. They react by digging their heels in and withholding their pee and poop in a desperate attempt to maintain their integrity.

Take, for example, TJ, whose parents had instituted a rule that he had to sit on the potty for five minutes at various junctures throughout the day (which is an eternity for young kids). One evening, TJ was sitting on the potty before bath and had not peed or pooped by the time the timer went off. His parents asked, "Are you sure you don't have to go?" He responded affirmatively. He then promptly arose and proceeded to pee right on the floor. This is not an uncommon scenario.

I also discourage picking up children to take them to the potty, especially in the middle of peeing or pooping, unless they have given you permission. This attempt to control the process can feel very intrusive to children and intensify their resistance to using the potty. Further, it sends that message that you know their body better than they do. If you see your child starting to strain or showing other signs of needing to eliminate, you might ask whether she would like help getting to the potty; but, if she says no, respect her wishes.

Punishing or shaming. By the time parents come to see me about a pottying problem, they are feeling completely helpless. Most are resorting to using punitive and shaming tactics. They may be comparing their child to other children or making threats about the consequences of not going on the potty, such as "Your brother was doing this by the time he was two and a half," or "Do you want to be the only one left in your class who uses pull-ups?" When you punish or shame children for accidents or for using a diaper instead of underwear, you are more likely to impede progress. Shame is a very powerful, toxic emotion that shuts children down. They get flooded with negative emotions that inhibit them from thinking clearly and learning from experience. They get paralyzed and can't move forward effectively in the process.

Using rewards. When it comes to potty learning, I find using rewards particularly problematic because children instinctively know that their parents are trying to control them. Have I mentioned that this dynamic tends to result in defiance and resistance rather than compliance? Further, the flip side of getting a reward is the disappointment children feel when they don't earn it. This makes pottying a source of stress and self-doubt.

Bootcamp. As you know by now, I am not a fan of boot camps. While they vary in their specific tactics, most of them entail children going bottomless for a few days while parents use intrusive methods to coax their children to use the toilet, such as making their children sit on the potty for periods of time at different junctures throughout the day and picking them up in the middle of peeing or pooping and placing them on the toilet. There is an intense focus on getting the child to cooperate with the parents' plan and expectations.

No doubt, this method works for some children. And, to be fair, my perspective is negatively skewed because so many families come to see me on the heels of an epic bootcamp fail, for example, this mom who recently wrote to me in a panic: "After a botched four-day potty training bootcamp that quickly devolved into a power struggle, we found ourselves at square one. . . . Unfortunately, we regrettably seem to have created some anxiety for [Zach]. . . . When he starts to have the feeling of needing to go, he has a mini freak-out. He whimpers, dances around, and wants to be picked up or sit in our lap. We feel awful for creating this angst for him (we definitely fell into the 'overprompting' trap) and don't want him to suffer."

For children like Zach, who fall into that category of the more sensitive, intense little ones who crave control, boot camp often backfires. It is a method that is clearly driven by the parents' agenda and thus leads to power struggles, increased anxiety, and often regression in the pottying process. For children who are more go with the flow (no pun intended) by nature, bootcamp may work fine, but why take the risk? When your child is ready and you have followed the steps above to support her to feel and be in charge of her body, she is much more likely to master this skill on her own.

Making toileting a social, playtime endeavor. To incentivize children to sit on the potty, many parents give in to demands for or voluntarily offer up screens for children to use or books for mom and dad to read to them while on the toilet. I discourage this because it sets children up to think that potty time is playtime, rather than simply elimination time. (I know, you're thinking it's the rare adult who isn't on his phone while doing his business, but adults aren't engaging in mastering a new skill when they're on the potty.) Kids then become dependent on being entertained on the toilet and may use it as a tool to get parental attention. "I'll sit on the potty if I can watch Daniel Tiger or Peppa Pig," is a frequent refrain I've heard. Young children are very strategic. They know how desperate their parents are for them to use the potty, and they exploit it (being strategic, not manipulative). One little girl announced that she would try to poop on the potty but that mom would have to come in and read to her. This went on for almost 30 minutes as her little brother got zero attention in the next room. Put that one in the win column for this clever little girl.

Constantly talking about the potty. If you focus too intensely on using the potty—constantly reminding or asking your child about whether he has to go or frequently reading books about going on the potty (when your child hasn't requested them)—it can increase resistance. Children pick up on the underlying meaning of your actions—that you are trying to control them. Further, the whole potty process takes over your everyday interactions, which tends to increase everyone's stress level and detracts from just enjoying your child.

FINAL NOTE

Potty learning challenges can be complex and confusing. As you can see from the stories above, they are often caused by underlying issues your child is struggling with. It is important to identify these root causes in order to come up with a successful plan around potty learning. Making the mindshift from thinking you have to train your child and assert control over his elimination to empowering him to be in charge of his body will enable you to support, rather than thwart, the process.

7

MEALTIME

Daniela and Marcel are very keen on making dinnertime family time; but their almost four-year-old, Reuben, resists sitting at the table for more than a few minutes. He keeps getting up to play. Daniela and Marcel try negotiation/bribery ("If you sit for five minutes and eat five bites of chicken and three of broccoli, you can have extra dessert"), threats ("No books before bed if you don't sit down and eat"), and logic ("You are going to be hungry if you don't eat enough").

None of these tactics is working, so they have started to allow Reuben to bring a tablet to the table and play games, despite the fact that they had sworn never to allow any screens during mealtimes. They feel very sad about the fact that a fair share of the precious time they have with Reuben at the end of the day is spent with him diverted by a screen, but they feel helpless to effect a change. Without the incentive of the tablet, they don't see how they can get Reuben to stay at the table for longer than two or three minutes. Even then, he is so distracted by the tablet that he still doesn't eat, which provokes further power struggles. Daniela and Marcel are at a loss as to how to turn this mealtime situation around to make it a healthy, joyful experience for all.

I see this dynamic play out in home after home: parents ensconced in battles to get their kids to sit at the table and eat a good meal.

There are a range of reasons a child might present difficulties around eating and mealtimes. One is that the child is a "discriminating" (also known as "picky") eater due to sensory issues. These kids have a heightened reaction to foods based on their texture or smell or, sometimes, even to the way the foods look. They reject them based on these aversions.

Children may also refuse a food because they have developed a negative association with it. For example, three-year-old Gavin would not go near any red foods because he had mistaken a sliver of red pepper for what he thought was a piece of candy. The disgust he experienced at the surprise of the savory versus sweet taste he was expecting led to his rejecting *all* red foods, even those he had previously enjoyed, such as strawberries and tomatoes. (Highly sensitive kids who are bigger reactors and tend to get fixed ideas about things are more likely to have this kind of reaction.)

Children might also be choosy about foods due to a motor/physiological problem. For example, some children don't have the muscle strength in their jaw to effectively chew hard, crunchy foods, so they insist on eating only soft, mushy foods that they can handle comfortably.

It is important to assess the root cause of your child's food-related challenge in order to respond in a way that most effectively encourages healthy eating. If you suspect that there is an underlying sensory or physiological issue at play, it is important to talk to your child's health care provider or a child development specialist. (To learn about more complex feeding issues, check out the resources in the appendix around how to understand and work with sensory-based feeding challenges.)

For the purpose of this chapter, I am going to stick to food and mealtime challenges that involve power struggles with children who don't have a sensory or other motor/physiological challenge and who generally enjoy a variety of healthy foods. With this group of kids, the mindset that most often leads to strategies that backfire and increase power struggles around food is parents *thinking they can and should make their children eat*—that this is something they can control. To try to get their children to eat, parents engage in all sorts of strategies. They try logic ("You'll be hungry if you don't eat enough breakfast"), threats ("There will be no TV if you don't eat your dinner"), or bribery/rewards ("You can have the tablet at the table if you stay for at least 15 minutes"). As you have seen in case after case described in previous chapters, the problem with all of these tactics is that they depend on your child ultimately taking the bribe or reward. What if she decides she's happy to give up TV or go to school hungry? One family just shared this one for the textbooks: After weeks of mealtime battles with three-year-old Maisy, they told her she had to go to her room and do nothing if she wasn't going to sit at the table and eat with them. They took her to her room and proceeded to take all the books and toys out while Maisy looked on with an impish grin (that drove her parents even more crazy). As they were leaving, Maisy, calm as a cucumber, pointed to a shelf and said, "Mommy, you forgot the stuffed animals." (In other words, "Knock yourselves out; you can't make me do anything!")

Most importantly, when children feel forced to eat, their knee-jerk reaction, based on the laws of self-preservation, is to show they can't be controlled: "You can't make me!" or "You're not the boss of me!" Their power is in proving to you that they, in fact, are in control. This leads to kids digging in their heels and ultimately eating less.

REUBEN: RESISTANCE TO FAMILY MEALTIME

The Mindsets and Mindshifts

When we take a step back to try to get some perspective on this mealtime dynamic, the first insight that emerges for Daniela and Marcel is that temperament is a big factor. Reuben is a feisty little guy who is fierce about having his way. He will go the distance to pursue his agenda, which often diverges from their agenda. Daniela and Marcel are both pleasers who don't like conflict. They are also older parents. They waited a long time to have a child. Their fantasy was that they would be a sympatico triad—that their child would be a compliant companion. They were not prepared for Reuben's intensity, nor for the power struggles that spirited (or highly sensitive) children are more likely to provoke when their agenda is thwarted and they can't have their way. They just want Reuben to be happy all the time. *They believe that being a happy child means the child is happy all the time.* This belief makes it especially hard for Daniela and Marcel to set the consistent limits and boundaries that big reactors like Reuben need in order to manage their strong emotions and desires. *They worry that the distress he experiences and expresses when he can't have his way is harmful to him; and that they are being "mean" and rejecting when they don't acquiesce to his demands.* In fact, when they try to give Reuben a specific direction, for example, to clean up his toys, he will often accuse them of shouting at him and being "unkind" when they are in fact using calm voices. (He just doesn't like that they are asking him to do something he is not interested in doing. Being corrected is uncomfortable for Reuben and this reaction almost always derails the process—his goal.) This has resulted in Daniela and Marcel *feeling uncomfortable being clear about directions because Reuben makes them feel like they are being harsh and dictatorial.*

Then, there is the whole specter of food, which is very anxiety-producing for Daniela and Marcel. This is especially true for Daniela, who comes from a culture and family where parents hand feed children at least until they are five or six and there is an expectation that plates will be cleaned. They have decided that they don't want to do the feeding; they want Reuben to be more independent and feed himself. That is what they do in his preschool and they want him to adapt to this cultural norm. But leaving it to Reuben to decide what he does and doesn't eat is making them very anxious. It puts them in the mindset that *they have to control Reuben's behavior to get him to eat.* The only tactic that gets him to the table is to give him the tablet, which they don't like doing but feel is the only choice.

Becoming aware of the mindsets at play that are creating the exact opposite of the pleasant, bonding experience they want mealtime to be, helps Daniela and Marcel make important mindshifts: *setting limits will be loving, not harmful for Reuben; the distress Reuben experiences when he can't have his way is tolerable stress that he can work through and grow from; trying to control his behavior is backfiring and leading to more, not fewer, power struggles; and providing clear directions and expectations is not being harsh and dictatorial but rather is an important parental responsibility.* They remind themselves that Reuben is good at taking instruction at school and accepting the countless limits that are imposed throughout the day. He tolerates it when he can't be the line leader and snack helper, which are his favorite jobs. He sits at the table for snack and accepts whatever is offered to eat. He adores his teacher, who is warm and also very clear about her expectations. He knows exactly what to do to be successful there. This insight emboldens Daniela and Marcel to do the hard work of getting out of their comfort zone and become the loving limit setters that Reuben needs them to be.

The Plan

Daniela and Marcel set a limit that there will be no screens at the table. They explain that the focus of mealtime is on filling their bodies with yummy, healthy foods and connecting and sharing. They outright acknowledge that they know he may not like this rule, but they are still going to implement it to diffuse the fight before it begins.

They make it clear that they will not be forcing him to sit at the table or to eat. It is his job to decide what foods he eats and how much his belly needs to be full. Only he knows that. They recall times when his belly was so hungry that he ate a big breast of chicken and 10 pieces of broccoli. Another night his belly wasn't so hungry; he had had a special snack at school late in the day so he only had room for a little bowl of pasta. Only he knows what his body needs.

They also explain that they are not going to play or interact with him during mealtime unless he is at the table, which is where the action is. If he wants their attention, he will get it at the table. They want him to know exactly what to expect so he can make the best decisions for himself.

They set a time limit on dinner to ensure there are clear boundaries that help Reuben make better choices. They show Reuben the visual timer and explain that it has a very important job because it lets him know exactly how much time he has to eat. When the timer beeps, it means dinner is over. So, if Reuben decides not to come to the table or to eat only a little, the food still goes away, and the next chance to eat is at breakfast. (As illustrated in the story about Lily who called out for food after lights-out in chapter 5 on sleep, some families feel more comfortable enforcing this limit if they offer a small snack before bed. This way, if their child has tested the limit and doesn't eat much or at all before the timer goes off at dinner, she still has a chance to eat something before bed.)

They decide to give Reuben more freedom around feeding himself. They want Reuben to ultimately use his utensils to eat; but, since they have recently stopped feeding him directly, they see that giving him space to get comfortable feeding himself in any way he likes is important. If he wants to use his hands and play with the food to get more familiar and comfortable with it, they will encourage that.

The Outcome

We implement this new plan on a home visit so I can support Daniela and Marcel in following through. They know themselves well.

They are worried that, while the plan sounds great in the comfort of my office, in the heat of the moment, their emotions will prevail. They will end up reverting to bribery, threats, and coaxing to get Reuben to come to the table and ultimately will cave on the use of the tablet.

The resistance starts even before the meal is put on the table. Marcel announces that dinner will be ready in five minutes. Reuben, not skipping a beat, responds: "My belly isn't hungry tonight. I'm fine." I use this as the perfect opportunity to set the stage for the new approach and do exactly the opposite of what Reuben is expecting—that his parents will jump in and start trying to convince him to come to the table and eat dinner. I respond: "Well, the great news, Reuben, is that it's your belly and only you know what it needs to feel happy and full. I don't know how your belly feels, do I? And you don't know how my belly feels—only I know that. *I'm* going to eat the yummy dinner your mommy and daddy have made because my belly is telling me it's hungry and it will be mad and growl at me if I don't fill it up. You have to decide what your belly needs. That's your choice."

Daniela and Marcel put dinner on the table, and Reuben immediately announces, "I'll come to the table if I can watch a show." Daniela responds: "That's not a choice, sweetie." Reuben retorts, "Well, I'm not coming then," and runs to the other side of the room, where he starts playing with his cars. Daniela and Marcel reflexively start to coax Reuben to the table: "Don't you want to show Claire how much you love avocado? Your belly is going to be mad if you don't eat any food." I step in: "Oh, Mom and Dad, remember, Reuben is a really smart kid and he is great at making smart decisions. He can see the timer and knows exactly how much time there is to eat dinner. If his belly is hungry or he wants to join our conversation, he can always choose to come to the table." I redirect them by suggesting that we each share a funny story about our day. Doing this dramatizes for Reuben that all the action is at the table. We keep up our animated discussion with lots of laughter and talk about how yummy the food is. Slowly, Reuben moves closer.

He eventually approaches the table. I signal to Daniela and Marcel not to get all excited or say anything about how happy they are that he is joining us. That may sound cold, but it is strategic. Reuben is in a stage where "giving in" to a parental request or agenda feels like ceding control—aka eating crow—which is what he is currently dead set against. If we make a big deal about his joining us, he is likely to run for the hills. Instead, we organically integrate him into the discussion by showing him silly food combinations, like dipping a piece of chicken into the avocado to see how that tastes. I ask whether he has any ideas for fun mixtures. Within minutes he is fully engaged and eating a great, healthy meal.

Naturally, given how different an approach this is for Daniela and Marcel, there are several moments when they revert to their knee-jerk coaxing: "Don't you want a few more pieces of the chicken that you love?" That is my cue to step in and reframe: "Oh, Mom and Dad, remember, Reuben knows what he needs. If he chooses to fill up his belly, it will be so happy. If he doesn't, then he'll have a big breakfast and tomorrow night he can decide to eat more at dinner."

Experiencing the success of this new approach, Daniela and Marcel have the motivation and muscle memory that helps them be consistent in implementing the plan we had established together. This changes the course of their meals, which is monumental, since dinnertime accounts for a major portion of their waking time together.

JULIA: THE PICKY EATER PROBLEM

Julia, age five, generally eats a pretty good range of healthy foods and her weight is on target. But she has preferences and is hesitant to try new foods. Her mom, Laurel, is a foodie and loves to cook. She spends a lot of time trying to coax and bribe Julia to try new foods or to accept foods she has enjoyed in the past but is now rejecting. The more Laurel tries to reason with Julia ("You loved broccoli last week; you couldn't get enough of it"), the more resistant Julia becomes. Laurel is getting increasingly frustrated. Mealtimes are becoming a source of stress, rather than a joyful time to connect.

The Mindsets and Mindshifts

As we analyze the dynamic at play, Julia quickly sees that the mindset that *she has to make Julia try new foods is backfiring because for Julia it's all about her need to feel in control.* The reason she avoids new foods is that they are unfamiliar to her. She doesn't know what to expect—what they will feel and taste like in her mouth. This makes her feel uncomfortable and out of control. She sticks to foods she knows because they are safe. *The more Laurel tries to convince or cajole Julia into trying new foods, the more avoidant Julia becomes.* Julia digs in her heels to resist being controlled, which makes it less likely she will try new foods.

Once Laurel makes this mindshift—*that she doesn't have the power to make Julia try new foods, nor is it helpful to force it*—she changes her focus from getting Julia to try new foods to creating opportunities for Julia to feel safe exploring the unfamiliar.

The Plan

Laurel stops trying to control Julia's eating. She no longer cajoles or tries to convince Julia to try new foods.

She gives Julia two plates at every meal. One plate is where she can put her preferred foods; the other plate is called the "learning plate,"[19] which is for foods Julia is still learning about and not yet ready to try. (The concept of the "learning plate" and other strategies for helping children get comfortable with new foods is from the SOS approach to feeding. Resources can be found in the appendix.)

She institutes family-style mealtimes. Laurel puts each food choice in a bowl, which they pass to each other. Julia takes a scoop of each food and either puts it on her main plate or her learning plate. This strategy is designed to expose Julia to other foods without feeling controlled or forced to try them.

She encourages exploration of new foods through a playful approach that helps Julia get comfortable with them. For example, she puts a carrot stick in her mouth and pretends it's a snake tongue. As she eats corn on the cob, she counts how many bites it takes to go from one end of the cob to the other. She gives Julia a child-safe knife to see how many pieces she can cut the chicken into. Laurel pretends she's a taste tester and dips veggie sticks (one of Julia's preferred foods) into different dips, such as yogurt, hummus, and guacamole. Laurel is careful never to cross the line to coax Julia to participate in the exploration. She is just modeling and making it fun to relieve the pressure that has been building at mealtimes which has become an obstacle to Julia's trying and enjoying new foods.

The Outcome

When Laurel stops trying to persuade Julia to eat and starts incorporating food exploration at mealtime, Julia becomes much more open to trying the foods on the learning plate. Laurel resists praising or even commenting when Julia starts to nibble at the new foods because she has found that this results in Julia's retreating. (It is amazing how tuned-in kids can be to their parents' ulterior motives at such a young age. They pick up on the fact that the praise is a method of control and parents saying "good job" and showing how happy they are about their child's behavior is designed to encourage more of that desired behavior. To maintain their sense of independence and agency, children who crave control may respond to praise by doing the opposite of what is expected.)

It turns out that this approach—creating opportunities for Julia to be exposed to and explore new foods without trying to cajole, convince, or force her—has also worked for other situations in which Julia is hesitant to try something new. For example, when Julia refuses to participate in a soccer class, Laurel refrains from the typical coaxing and bribing she used to do to get Julia to join the group. Instead, Laurel tells Julia that her commitment is to show up. Beyond that, it is up to Julia to decide to participate or not. After a few sessions of just watching, without Laurel pushing her to join, Julia slowly starts to get involved and ends up loving the activity.

MATHIUS: BARGAINING FOR "ONE MORE BITE"

Duane and Melanie are trapped in daily food battles with their four-year-old, Mathius, over whether he has eaten enough growing foods to have a sweet dessert. Dinnertime is consumed by Mathius's constantly announcing that he's ready for dessert while his parents demand that he take "one more bite." He nibbles at a piece of food and insists that this qualifies. Duane and Melanie find themselves debating whether this meets their criteria. They eventually get worn down and give in, albeit with a good dose of annoyance at Mathius for manipulating them (they call him a "cunning mastermind") and putting them in the position of having to cave on limits they think are important. "How is it that this little guy is essentially calling the shots?"

The major mindset Duane and Melanie are stuck in is *trying to change Mathius's behavior*—to get him to agree to eat more growing foods so they don't have to deal with the inevitable battle over dessert. This approach isn't getting them to their goal. And their *interpretation of his behavior as being manipulative*—that he is forcing them to give him what he desires—leads to anger and frustration. This only fuels the power struggle and interferes in Duane's and Melanie's ability to think clearly about the situation and make a better plan.

Once they accept that they *can't rule Mathius's behavior and that he is just being strategic to get his way*, Duane and Melanie are positioned to set and enforce limits they actually have the power to control. They can't make him eat more growing foods, but they *can* limit sweets, even if he doesn't like it.

The Plan

Duane and Melanie make it clear to Mathius what constitutes sufficient growing food intake. To get out of the "gray zone" that ensues when there is no clarity around whether Mathius has had a sufficient amount of growing foods, Duane and Melanie purchase a plate for Mathius that has dividers, with one large and two smaller compartments. In the large compartment, they put a manageable portion of growing foods. (They start with the minimum they feel is acceptable. For some kids, having too much food on their plate feels overwhelming, and they reject it all.) In the two smaller compartments, they put additional portions of the growing foods in case he wants more. They don't want to limit his intake of healthy foods; they just want to be crystal clear about how much growing food is sufficient to qualify for a sweet without creating a "clean plate club," to get out of constant bargaining for "two more bites." They clearly explain to Mathius that the large section of the plate contains the "minimum growing food" that he needs to grow healthy and strong.

They set a limit on dessert that comes as a natural consequence of eating sufficient healthy food (or not). If Mathius finishes all the food in the large compartment of his plate, he can have a sweet dessert. If he doesn't finish all the food in that compartment, he can choose a fresh fruit after dinner, not a sweet treat. These are his two great choices. He is the decider.

The Outcome

Initially, Mathius protests and tries to draw his parents back into a power struggle. But with a plan in place that they feel good about and can control, Duane and Melanie are able to stay firm, calm, and loving even in the face of Mathius's threats ("I'll never eat a growing food again if you don't give me the cookies!"). When he doesn't finish the growing foods in the large compartment and refuses the fruit choices, they respond: "No problem, that's up to you. If you change your mind and decide you'd like some fruit, let us know." When they don't react to his protests and he sees they are standing firm, he ultimately choses a fruit. After two nights of implementing the plan, he understands the new deal in the house and starts eating all the growing foods or accepts a fruit for dessert without a fight.

LUCY: FICKLE FRENZY

Three-year-old Lucy asks for toast for breakfast. Her mom, Samantha, presents it to her, but, uh-oh, she has cut it on the diagonal when Lucy wanted it halved down the middle! Lucy insists Samantha make a new piece of toast. Samantha sighs heavily—they've been around this block before: Lucy making what she sees as insane demands. Samantha looks at her partner, Tatiana, with that "what do I do?" shrug of the shoulders. They are exhausted from battles like this, which can be precipitated by seemingly minor issues. It's the same piece of bread whether it's cut one way or the other, but they are stressed by Lucy's distress and want to end everyone's misery. So Tatiana pops another piece of bread into the toaster. When she hands it to Lucy, Lucy announces that what she really wants is a scrambled egg. Tatiana gets increasingly annoyed with Lucy and tells her to make up her mind. Lucy shouts, "Stop telling me that! You're not the boss of me!" Tatiana responds, "Oh, yes, I am! That's it; just eat the toast and we're done." Lucy starts to pout and tells Tatiana to stop yelling at her, adding, "You're not being a kind mommy right now." Tatiana feels bad for losing it with Lucy and proceeds to whip up an egg.

The Mindsets and Mindshifts

The foundational faulty mindset at play for Samantha and Tatiana is that *Lucy should be able to act more rationally and is purposefully driving them insane.* Because she understands logic and is so verbal and bright, they expect Lucy to act more rationally, and they are angry at her for being so unreasonable. Their negative state of mind is exacerbated by *Lucy's inflammatory statements about their not being the boss of her, which they take at face value and assign malicious intent to.* Their reactivity only increases the power struggles.

At the same time, Samantha and Tatiana worry that *experiencing stress is damaging to Lucy.* When Samantha and Tatiana see Lucy in distress, they are triggered into reactive mode. On the one hand, while they think she is being totally irrational, *they also worry that her level of distress over these seemingly minor issues is harmful to her.* It then follows that they feel they are *being mean by not relieving Lucy's discomfort.* What's the big deal in giving her a new piece of toast or an alternate breakfast? They don't want to make her eat something she doesn't want.

All of these ambivalent feelings are making it very hard for Samantha and Tatiana to change course to right their ship and help Lucy be more flexible. Making the following mindshifts enables them to steer a new and healthier path. It begins with thinking about the root of Lucy's big reactions. She is sensitive and intense by nature. She tends to develop fixed ideas about how things should be and has a hard time when something doesn't happen exactly as she expects, be it the way her toast needs to be cut or which parent comes to get her out of bed in the morning. It is stressful for her when these expectations aren't met (as irrational as that may seem) and she can't cope. These insights shift Samantha and Tatiana away from *seeing Lucy's behavior as inappropriate and purposefully designed to drive them insane to gaining understanding that Lucy gets overwhelmed by her big emotions and needs their help to learn to be more flexible.*

This mindshift leads to other mindshifts—*that experiencing distress at not getting what she wants is not harmful to Lucy and they are not being mean when they set appropriate limits. Just because Lucy says she "needs" something doesn't mean that what she is demanding is necessarily good for her.* Samantha and Tatiana see that to help Lucy be more flexible, they will need to stick to important limits. This will mean tolerating the discomfort Lucy is likely to experience during the process of learning that she can handle it when things don't happen exactly the way she wants. They also now understand that when Lucy gets herself into these tizzies, she can't make a decision because she is out of sorts. Following her down this path is not helpful. What Lucy is not asking for but what she needs in these moments are more boundaries, not fewer. Without limits to guide her behavior, she spirals further out of control, which is decidedly not good for her.

Finally, they see that *Lucy does not harbor malicious intent when she hurls inflammatory statements at them.* She is acting on her emotions and trying to get back to her place of comfort—to have things go exactly as she thinks she needs them to be. There is nothing wrong with that. She is just trying to cope. Reacting harshly to these kinds of statements only reinforces them and gives them validity. This insight helps Samantha and Tatiana avoid falling into the trap of allowing these provocative proclamations to derail them from implementing the important limits and boundaries Lucy needs.

The Plan

They create a "breakfast book." Together with Lucy, Samantha and Tatiana make an activity out of taking lots of photos of Lucy eating all sorts of breakfast foods she enjoys. They print them out and put them in a basket. Each morning at breakfast, they show her two of the photos that depict her breakfast options for that day. She chooses which one she wants. They acknowledge that this is an important decision because, once she makes her choice, they are going to be sticking to it no matter what. They give her a minute to think carefully about which option she wants. (Some parents opt to do this the night before, having their child choose their breakfast before they go to sleep to avoid any issues in the morning.)

They engage Lucy in making breakfast. To give Lucy some control over the food, once Lucy chooses her breakfast, they offer her the option to help put it together so that it can be the way she likes. She can help cut toast the way she wants or put the eggs on the plate so they aren't too close to the strawberries—a pet peeve of hers.

They set a clear, final limit. Samantha and Tatiana are very clear that, once the food is ready, there will be no changes. If Lucy chooses not to eat the breakfast, over which they have given her a lot of control, no problem. They will never force her to eat. Like Adam and Brian did with Sadie (in chapter 2, on cooperation), they let Lucy know that they will put the food in a to-go container in case she gets hungry later.

The Outcome

Not surprisingly, the first morning they enact this plan, Lucy says she doesn't like any of the choices and blurts out, "I am going to tell you your choices!" Knowing that this is an attempt to gain control of the situation and that a big reaction will only derail them, Samantha and Tatiana remain calm and don't respond to Lucy's provocative statement. They let Lucy know that, since it's a big decision, they are going to give her a whole minute to think about it. When the minute is up, Lucy still insists that they are not the boss of her and none of the choices are okay! Samantha and Tatiana tell her that they will go ahead then and make eggs. She shouts, "That is the worst idea I ever heard!" Lucy then announces that she hates eggs (one of her favorite foods), will never eat them, and that they should not put them anywhere near her.

Samantha places the plate of Lucy's eggs on the counter and lets her know that it is her choice whether or not she wants to eat them. Samantha and Tatiana proceed to eat their breakfast, ignoring Lucy's continued provocations but not ignoring *her*. They tell funny stories and keep an upbeat tone to show Lucy that they are not angry and they are going to continue enjoying their breakfast (and will not let her throw them off course). They don't say another word about the eggs.

Within a few minutes, Lucy gets up and retrieves the plate of eggs and sheepishly starts to nibble at them. Samantha and Tatiana have learned not to make a big deal when Lucy starts to do what they have been angling for. No exclamations such as "What a good decision you've made!" or "We're so glad you came to the table!" While that may sound counterintuitive—why wouldn't you want to acknowledge a good decision a child has made?—as noted earlier, some children, especially those who are highly sensitive, have their antennae up for feeling controlled. When parents make a big deal in these situations, these children perceive it as a loss of control; that they have given in and their parents have won, which can reignite their defiance.

With Samantha and Tatiana following the same plan every mealtime, the breakfast battles end. It's not that Lucy always accepts what they are offering or that she stops making unreasonable demands. But by not getting reactive, and sticking to the plan they have established, Samantha and Tatiana are able to stay calm, loving, and in charge, which makes all the difference. They start to apply the same approach in other situations in which Lucy is being inflexible and are seeing great results. Lucy is becoming more adaptable, more regulated, and much happier, as are Samantha and Tatiana.

MASON: TREAT TERRORIST

Mason is a fierce and persistent four-year-old. He knows what he wants and pursues his goals with gusto. This attribute has enabled him to master many challenges, including learning to ride a two-wheeler at his very young age and swimming without floaties.

Mason is equally as persistent about accessing the foods he wants as he is about conquering new physical feats. He goes into the refrigerator and takes out what he wants instead of the food that his dad, Bernard, has prepared for him. He carries chairs over to the kitchen counter to get into the cabinets where the treats are, regardless of Bernard's rule that there is no climbing on counters and sweet treats are only for after dinner.

Bernard has made lots of threats, to the tune of, "there will be no snacks for the rest of the week if you climb back on that counter," which don't deter Mason. He just laughs mischievously as he continues his climb, which freaks Bernard out. He finds it chilling that this little person is laughing in his face and totally disrespecting him. Fuming, Bernard ultimately finds himself forcefully grabbing Mason from the counter and putting him in a chair to take a time-out. But persistent Mason keeps getting up, as if he couldn't care less about his father's limits. Bernard is distraught. He feels he has no way to control this "feral" child who is like a "heat-seeking missile" when he has a plan in mind. Time after time, Bernard ends up worn down and giving in: "Fine. You can have one cookie before dinner and that's it." But, once the meal is done, Mason is back at the counter seeking more cookies, which provokes yet another power struggle over sweets.

The Mindsets and Mindshifts

The first stumbling block for Bernard is seeing Mason as *purposefully misbehaving, that he should be able to assert greater self-control.* This is infuriating to Bernard and results in his responding with frustration and anger. Another mindset that's at play is *Bernard feeling that he needs to make Mason change his behavior,* which perpetuates the power struggle as Bernard tries to convince Mason to cooperate with the limits. Mason's refusal to do so leaves Bernard in an angry, resentful place that impedes his ability to think clearly about an alternative plan.

Add to the mix *Mason's mischievous laughing, which Bernard finds maddening and interprets as sociopathic.* Bernard worries that there is something deeply wrong with Mason because he has no respect for authority. This makes him very anxious, which quickly morphs into anger at Mason for behaving in such worrisome ways. This harsh reaction ultimately makes Bernard's tactics ineffective.

Once Bernard is conscious of these mindsets and the role they are playing in perpetuating this current dynamic, he is able to make these important mindshifts: While Mason is not following the rules, *he is not misbehaving. He is doing what is developmentally appropriate for a four-year-old— pursuing his goals using any strategies that work.* Bernard can't rely on Mason to one day decide "It really would be best for me not to eat so many sweets, so please limit my access to them." This leads to another mindshift—that *trying to convince Mason to stop seeking treats is not an effective plan because that puts Bernard in the position of having to wait for Mason to decide to change his behavior.* Bernard needs to make a plan to prevent Mason from engaging in unhealthy behavior that *Bernard has the power to implement.*

Finally, *Bernard is relieved to discover that Mason is not a sociopath; his laughter in the heat of these power struggles is not fraught with malicious intent.* It is impossible to know exactly what is behind Mason's laughter, but it is likely due to his being on overdrive and highly stimulated by this cat-and-mouse game. Further, his ability to outwit his dad may be inducing mixed feelings. On the one hand, it makes him feel powerful. On the other hand, it can be scary for kids to be in charge. They need their parents to be in control in order to feel safe, even if their actions belie this. Struggling with these complex feelings can be uncomfortable for children and can result in anxious behaviors such as "devious" laughter.

Bernard now sees that the most loving response is to get back into control in a positive way. This means not reacting to and getting derailed by provocative behavior, which only reinforces the power Mason feels in outwitting him.

The Plan

Bernard talks with Mason about all the ways his persistence is awesome. He recalls with Mason a number of situations in which he has muscled through a challenge and how this persistence has led to his developing so many skills. Bernard wants to reinforce this amazing attribute.

He acknowledges and accepts that Mason doesn't like it when he can't get something he wants. Bernard acknowledges that, just like Mason pursues other goals with gusto, he puts the same effort into getting the foods he wants. Bernard completely understands that desire.

He explains that deciding what food will be for mealtime and how many snacks he can have is Daddy's job. Bernard emphasizes that it is his job to make sure Mason stays strong and healthy. So even though Mason might want to go to the refrigerator during mealtime to pick out different foods, or have a lot of snacks throughout the day, Bernard can't allow that. He is sure to tell Mason that he doesn't expect him to like these rules and that he is not asking him to agree with them. (Remember, if you are trying to convince your child to agree with your limit, you are likely to land in the gray zone when your child picks up on the fact that you are counting on his concurrence.)

Bernard establishes a plan he can implement. Every Sunday, they will make their menus for the week. Mason will help plan them and have choices within the limits Bernard sets, such as whether they will have carrots or broccoli for their vegetable.

Once the meals are set, they will be sticking to them. There is no going into the refrigerator or climbing up to cabinets to access other foods. He explains that if Mason has a hard time following this rule, Bernard will be a helper and put locks on the fridge and junk food cabinet.

There will be two times a day when Mason can choose a treat, after lunch and after dinner.

Bernard creates a basket of healthy foods that Mason can access whenever he wants to give Mason some agency and to ensure that he never goes hungry.

The Outcome

Mason loves making the menus and helping with the shopping. Bernard is thrilled and thinks he is home free. But, then, at their first dinner under this new system, Mason immediately goes to the pantry to get some Ritz crackers—his obsession. He would fill himself up on them given the chance. Bernard gives Mason one reminder: if he chooses to take the crackers, Daddy will help him follow the rule and will put the lock on the cabinet. Mason, with that impish grin, pauses as if contemplating his choices. Then, he grabs the crackers. Bernard, as gently and calmly as he can, extricates the crackers from Mason's hand, puts them back in the pantry, and secures a lock on the door. He goes back to the table and continues with the meal. Mason pouts and tells Bernard that he won't be eating any dinner if he can't have the crackers. Bernard lovingly responds that it is Mason's body and only he can decide whether he eats any dinner or not. Bernard suggests that maybe Mason should listen to his belly and see what it thinks. Will it be okay if it doesn't get any food until breakfast? Bernard then starts talking to *his* belly and announces: "My belly says it needs a little more of this chicken because you did such a good job pouring the sauce on it, which makes it taste so good." Bernard doesn't react to Mason's threats or pouts, but he doesn't ignore him. He continues to be silly. He makes a game of closing his eyes and tasting bites of different foods to see whether his belly can guess what they are. Slowly, Mason starts to eat some of his dinner.

The situation repeats when it comes to the junk food cabinet. Mason tests the limit. Bernard calmly picks him up off the counter and puts a lock on the cabinet. This leads to a meltdown. Bernard acknowledges that Mason is unhappy with the rule. He lets Mason know what his choices are at that moment: yogurt or a piece of fruit. Mason is too upset to process this. Bernard responds: "If you change your mind and decide you want the fruit or yogurt, let me know." Once Mason sees that Bernard is not going to cave on the limit, nor is he going to react to his meltdown, he calms down and chooses strawberries.

After a few days of further testing and Bernard staying calm and loving while remaining clear about the limits, the food battles became fewer and farther between.

STRATEGIES FOR ESTABLISHING
HEALTHY EATING HABITS

Here are some key strategies for avoiding battles around food. To dig deeper into how to nurture a healthy eater, see the resources on this topic in the appendix.

Create routines around mealtime. Everyone might share something funny that happened during the day or the highlight of their week. You might play guessing games, such as 20 questions. Share stories about your experiences growing up, which kids get such a kick out of. Routines make children feel loved and secure. They also help children look forward to each meal.

Get clear on the division of responsibility when it comes to mealtime. You and your child each have a job. Yours is to provide him with healthy food choices and pleasant meal and snack times. It is your child's job to decide which of these healthy foods to eat and how much to eat. When you approach feeding this way, your child learns to listen to his body and make healthy food choices. It also leads to fewer power struggles between parent and child around food (from the work of Ellyn Satter[20]).

Engage your child in developing menus for the week. Have her help you find the ingredients at the grocery store.

Explore new foods through play. Engage your child in meal preparation. Let him be a taste tester. Make eating fun. Give your child a child-safe knife and suggest he cut up his avocado into different shapes and sizes (but not suggesting he do the same; the power is in the modeling). You do it as well, and then go ahead and eat the shape you've made. You can make a game of counting the pieces as you cut them and put them in your mouth. Explore and be playful. Resist coaxing, cajoling, or bribing your child to eat. Any indication that you have an agenda and are invested in his eating can result in resistance, especially for children who are all about having the control.

What to Avoid

Forcing your child to eat. Eating is all about self-regulation—children learning to read their body's cues as to when they are hungry and full. That is what leads to healthy eating habits in the long term. Forcing your child to eat sends the message to him that he doesn't know his own body and that he always needs to rely on others to tell him how much to eat and what his body is feeling and needs. And, as the stories above elucidate, you can't actually make your children eat. That is something only they can decide to do. Using all those tactics to try to control a child's intake only leads to power struggles and their eating less, not more.

Nagging or making deals with your child. Strategies such as "Just two more bites" or "If you eat your vegetables, you will get dessert" don't work in the long run. Children who learn to make deals about eating quickly learn to make deals and ask for rewards for doing other things, such as brushing their teeth or cleaning up their toys.

Screens at the table. Most parents I talk to don't want their kids on screens at mealtimes. It's something they swore they would never allow. They want meals to be a time to connect, without distractions. Then, reality strikes, and they are faced with a child who resists coming to the table. Suddenly, their best laid plans go out the window. They see the screen as the only tool at their disposal to get their child to eat, be it allowing him to have a tablet at the table or eating in front of the TV. (One family calls it "the path of least resistance parenting.") As you have seen from the stories in this book, it is possible to set limits around screens that children will adapt to *if you stick to them*. As hard as it might be to withstand your child's vehement protests, the payoff is big. Research[21] clearly shows that families who establish and implement very clear limits around screen time have far fewer power struggles in the long term around screen use, with significant benefits for children and parents. (See the resources on screen time in the appendix.)

FINAL THOUGHTS

As you can see, the same rules apply for mealtime as they do for establishing healthy sleep, helping children master potty learning, responding to tantrums, and reducing aggressive behavior. It's all about getting clear on what you do and don't control, setting clear expectations that are developmentally appropriate, showing empathy for your child's feelings and experience, providing the tools he needs, and communicating your confidence in him to master whatever hurdle or limit he is facing.

This is a good segue to the conclusion of this book, which distills all the learning from the stories in these chapters to home in on what exactly your job is.

8

YOUR JOB

When I reflect on my work with families over the past three decades and on my own parenting journey, I have come to the conclusion that there are two overarching responsibilities we have as parents: to be responsive, not reactive, and to be our children's helpers, not their fixers or rescuers. These jobs are deeply intertwined.

To do these jobs well, mindset matters, a lot. You need to see that your children aren't acting out (misbehaving) on purpose; that they don't have the ability to control their impulses or manage life's stressors effectively or efficiently yet; that they are driven to go for what they want and aren't being manipulative but strategic; that feelings are not right or wrong, good or bad—that a full range of emotions is part of being human; that tantrums aren't inherently harmful to children; and that your child is way more competent than you may think he is. He can learn to cope with not being with you every waking (or sleeping!) second and not getting everything he wants, when he wants it. He can learn to muscle through a challenging task and adapt to changes in his world. Once you have mastered these mindsets, you are best positioned to help your children learn and grow by setting loving limits with empathy, patience, respect, and support for the hard work they are undertaking to adapt to a complex world. It starts with being responsive.

RESPONSIVE VERSUS REACTIVE PARENTING

Caring for young children (really, children of any age) is an intensely emotional experience. We love our kids so deeply and want the best for them so that, when faced with an incident or behavior that we worry is detrimental to their well-being, we get reactive. We are triggered into a (sometimes highly) emotional state that often results in the exact opposite outcome from what we are aiming for. It escalates the situation at hand; reduces the chance for a successful outcome; and increases stress for ourselves and our children, as the stories in this book illustrate. Being reactive is one of the greatest obstacles to our ability to be in control and able to set and enforce appropriate limits while remaining loving and positively connected to our children.

The antidote to reactive parenting is *responsive parenting*. This means taking a step back to think about what we know about our children and what we think their behavior is communicating. This requires mindfulness—the ability to calm our minds and bodies when we get triggered by a challenging behavior. This state of mind enables us to think about our feelings and reactions and then choose a response that we believe (and hope!) is going to teach our children positive ways to get their needs met or to cope with whatever challenge they are facing—precisely the process the families in this book engaged in. For example, Audrey and Stephen, who moved from reactivity in the face of their children's roughhousing after lights-out to responsivity by baking in time for their kids to engage in this active play at a more reasonable time in the routine. Or Nikki, who moved from being reactive to her daughter's demands that she sleep with her by getting angry and resentful, to being responsive by establishing a bedtime routine that included uninterrupted time for bonding but a clear limit at lights-out.

Because it is so hard to be responsive in the moment when you are triggered, it is important to get comfortable taking your own time-out when your child is provoking a situation. "Sportscast" what's at play: "I have asked you to stop throwing mulch. You are having a hard time following this direction. I am going to take a mommy moment to think about how I can help you solve this problem." Taking this time gives you a chance to calm down so you can think through the best way to respond and prevents you from falling into the deadly "gray zone," in which you are trying to get your child to comply with a direction or limit with no clear end game. (Sometimes, it also stops kids short in their tracks because they are so shocked at your calm response!) Taking this time-out can keep you from being reactive, gives you time to think, and provides a very powerful model for exercising self-control. It is also a great tool for co-parents as a way to avoid undermining each other (one parent says no, while the other caves) and to allow time to come up with a united plan. You announce that the adults are going to have a mommy/daddy meeting and will be back in a minute to let your child know what his choices are (that, remember, are ones you can actually enforce!). "You cannot throw the mulch. We can help you find something else that is safe to play with, or it will be time to come inside."

This approach enables you to be responsive, not reactive, and is as important for you as it is for your child, because it prevents you from acting in ways you feel bad about and regret. It also helps your child learn to make good choices and to become a good problem solver, one of the most important attributes for success socially and academically far, far into the future.

HELPER VERSUS PROBLEM SOLVER

When you are in a responsive state of mind, you are well positioned to be your child's helper—to empower her to solve the myriad challenges she will face as she makes her way through this world. Your job is not to be her fixer or rescuer—to make the difficult feelings go away or solve a problem she is struggling with. You have seen this theme reverberate in the stories told throughout these pages: when a dad was able to avoid a power struggle and stay calm and loving in the heat of the moment by giving his child a choice between climbing into a car seat on his own or having him be a helper to place him in securely; when a mom stepped in as a helper by escorting her daughter back to her room when she kept running out after lights-out; and when a dad held himself back from trying to make it all better when his child was struggling to learn to ride a scooter independently and, instead, acted as a helper to guide his child through the problem to find his own solution.

Being your child's helper means finding that fine, but critically important, line between *supporting*—providing the information, tools, and encouragement your child needs to solve a problem—and *enabling*—doing something for your child that she can do for herself. This entails assessing the difference between what your child *wants* versus what she *needs*. Your child may be struggling with a puzzle and *want* you to put the pieces in the correct spaces, but does she *need* you to do this? In the long run, would it be better for your child to have you fix her problem and reduce her frustration, or to be her helper and guide her through a series of steps to build her skills and confidence that she can master this challenge?

Your child may call out to you after lights-out that he *wants* you to rearrange his blankets again, but does he *need* you to do this? Would it be better for him to have you come into his room repeatedly and set a pattern that delays his getting to sleep, or to be his helper and teach him how to do it himself, boosting his confidence to solve his own problems and putting an end to nightly power struggles?

Seeing yourself as a helper also puts you in a mindset to lovingly set limits. You let your child know that, if he throws a dangerous object, you will be a helper and put that object away to keep him safe. Rather than shouting at or making threats when your child refuses to "freeze" at the crosswalk, you are a helper and calmly pick her up to secure her safely in the stroller. When your child grabs a toy out of the hands of his new baby sister, you give him a choice of handing the object back himself or having you be a helper and return it to its rightful user. No shaming, punishments, or rewards are necessary—just clear boundaries and support to learn to make good decisions as he grows.

The insights I have gained about the power of parental mindsets guide me, too, as I continue to work toward being the best parent I can be to my children, now in their late twenties. Truth be told, rarely a day goes by that I don't feel the sting of regret at how much less anxious and reactive I might have been when my kids were growing up, how much calmer and less stressed I would have been, and how much more joy I would have experienced, had I been more aware of the faulty mindsets in my own head. I wish I had understood that having a happy child doesn't mean he's happy all the time, and that learning to deal with life's frustrations and disappointments involves children feeling uncomfortable and unhappy at times. Making my own mindshifts, albeit long after my kids were out of toddlerhood, has enabled me to better equip them to muscle through the challenges they face and to trust them to solve their own problems and make good choices. So, when parents ask me if it's too late for their child, fearing they've already "ruined" him (even at the ripe age of three), I can tell them the good news: it's never too late.

APPENDIX

Adapting to a New Baby

Lerner Child Development: https://www.lernerchilddevelopment
.com/arrival-of-new-sibling

Door Helpers

Safety knob covers: https://amzn.to/34IEIQ6
Door-securing devices: https://amzn.to/3oLuO8m

Early Brain Development

Siegel, Daniel J., Tina Payne Bryson, and OverDrive Inc. *The Whole-Brain Child: 12 Revolutionary Strategies to Nurture Your Child's Developing Mind*. New York: Random House, 2011.

Delahooke, Mona. *Beyond Behaviors: Using Brain Science and Compassion to Understand and Solve Children's Behavioral Challenges*. Eau Claire, WI: PESI.

Early Intervention Services

"What You Need to Know: Early Intervention": https://bit.ly
/34LR89S

Feeding

Sensory-based feeding challenges: https://sosapproachtofeeding
.com/

Eat and Feed with Joy (Ellyn Satter): https://www.ellynsatter
institute.org/

Playing Parental Favorites

Lerner Child Development: https://www.lernerchilddevelopment
.com/mainblog/go-away-mommy-daddy-reads-to-me-coping
-with-parental-preferences

Potty Learning

Squatty potty: https://amzn.to/2HXt8aH

"The Poo in You" (video that explains what happens when you
hold in bowel movements): https://bit.ly/3ehZf0R

Sensory Processing/Calming Strategies

Online Resources:

Understood.org: https://www.understood.org/search-results/v1
/search?query=sensory+processing

TeeKozkids: https://teekozkids.com

STAR Institute: https://www.spdstar.org/

Wiggle seat: https://www.lakeshorelearning.com/products/class
room-furniture/chairs-seating/flex-space-wobble-cushions/p
/LC511/?utm_source=google&utm_medium=ppc&utm_cam
paign=nbdsa&gclid=Cj0KCQiAgomBBhDXARIsAFNyUqN
ttvrqwrR_x5sI3iWXtCd38cQbEwrebP3NTadyjlcai6mCxOn
--BEaAmD

Heavy work/calming tools: https://funandfunction.com/?utm
_medium=search&gclid=Cj0KCQjwrfvsBRD7ARIsAKuDvM
M7S8-lqzSGeK045uR1BsQK1vQJ-zsu3hZW2saQIy9W1aHd
-863l10aAvufEALw_wcB

Books:

Kranowitz, Carol Stock. *The Out-of-Sync Child: Recognizing and
Coping with Sensory Processing Disorder*. New York: A Skylight
Press Book/A Perigee Book, 2005.

Screen Time

ZERO TO THREE's Screen Sense: https://www.zerotothree.
org/resources/series/screen-sense

Sleep
>   Okay to wake clocks (Do an online search; there are many to choose from)

Sleep training myths:
>   Kansagra, Sujay. "Sleep Training Your Child: Myths and Facts Every Parent Should Know." Published June 1, 2017. https://pediatrics.duke.edu/news/sleep-training-your-child-myths-and-facts-every-parent-should-know.

Temperament
Online Resources:
>   Understanding and supporting highly sensitive children: https://www.lernerchilddevelopment.com/highly-sensitive-children
>   ZERO TO THREE: https://www.zerotothree.org/search?q=temperament

Books:
>   Boyce, Thomas A. *The Orchid and the Dandelion: Why Some Children Struggle and How All Can Thrive.* New York: Knopf, 2019.
>   Kurcinka, Mary Sheedy. *Raising Your Spirited Child: A Guide for Parents Whose Child Is More Intense, Sensitive, Perceptive, Persistent, and Energetic.* Third Edition. New York: William Morrow, 2015.

Timers
>   Visual timers: https://www.amazon.com/visual-timer/s?k=visual+timer

Toddlerhood
>   Klein, Tovah. *How Toddlers Thrive.* New York: Touchstone, 2015.
>   Lieberman, A. F. *The Emotional Life of the Toddler.* New York: Free Press, 1993.

NOTES

1. Mary K. Rothbart and Brad E. Sheese, "Temperament and Emotion Regulation," in *Handbook of Emotion Regulation*, ed. J. J. Grossion (New York: The Guildford Press, 2007), 331–50.

2. W. Thomas Boyce, *The Orchid and the Dandelion: Why Some Children Struggle and How All Can Thrive* (New York: Knopf, 2019).

3. Angela Prencipe and Phillip David Zelazo, "Development of Affective Decision Making for Self and Other: Evidence for the Integration of First- and Third-Person Perspectives," *Psychological Science* (July 2005): 501–5, https://doi.org/10.1111/j.0956-7976.2005.01564.x.

4. Daniel J. Siegel and Tina Payne Bryson, *The Whole-Brain Child: 12 Revolutionary Strategies to Nurture Your Child's Developing Mind* (New York: Random House Digital, Inc., 2011).

5. Daniel Hughes, Jonathan Baylin, and Daniel J. Siegel, *Brain-Based Parenting: The Neuroscience of Caregiving for Healthy Attachment* (New York: W. W. Norton & Company, Inc., 2012).

6. National Scientific Council on the Developing Child, "Excessive Stress Disrupts the Architecture of the Developing Brain: Working Paper 3 Updated Edition" (2005, 2009, 2014), accessed October 31, 2020, http://www.developingchild.harvard.edu.

7. Dictionary.com, "Cooperation," accessed on October 31, 2020, https://www.dictionary.com/browse/cooperation.

8. Elizabeth R. Sowell et al., "*In Vivo* Evidence for Post-Adolescent Brain Maturation in Frontal and Striatal Regions," *Nature Neuroscience* 2, no. 10: (October 1999): 859–61, https://pubmed.ncbi.nlm.nih.gov/10491602/.

9. National Scientific Council on the Developing Child, "Excessive Stress Disrupts the Architecture of the Developing Brain."

10. Siegel and Bryson, *The Whole-Brain Child*.

11. Leah Kuypers, "The Zones of Regulation," accessed October 31, 2020, https://www.zonesofregulation.com/index.html.

12. Hyeonjin Jeon and Seung-Hwan Lee, "From Neurons to Social Beings: Short Review of the Mirror Neuron System Research and Its Socio-Psychological and Psychiatric Implications," *Clinical Psychopharmacology and Neuroscience: The Official Scientific Journal of the Korean College of Neuropsychopharmacology* 16, no. 1 (February 2018): 18–31, https://doi.org/10.9758/cpn.2018.16.1.18.

13. Prencipe and Zelazo, "Development of Affective Decision Making for Self and Other."

14. Sowell et al., "*In Vivo* Evidence for Post-Adolescent Brain Maturation in Frontal and Striatal Regions."

15. Lucy Jane Miller, *Sensational Kids: Hope and Help for Children With Sensory Processing Disorder* (New York: Penguin Press, 2014), 249–50.

16. Paula L. Ruttle et al., "Disentangling Psychobiological Mechanisms Underlying Internalizing and Externalizing Behaviors in Youth: Longitudinal and Concurrent Associations with Cortisol," *Hormones and Behavior* 59, no. 1 (July 2011): 123, DOI: 10.1016/j.yhbeh.2010.10.015.

17. Michael Gradisar et al., "Behavioral Interventions for Infant Sleep Problems: A Randomized Controlled Trial," *Pediatrics* 137, no. 6 (June 2016), https://doi.org/10.1542/peds.2015-1486.

18. Melissa Wake et al., "Five-Year Follow-up of Harms and Benefits of Behavioral Infant Sleep Intervention: Randomized Trial," *Pediatrics* 130, no. 4 (October 2012): 643–51, https://doi.org/10.1542/peds.2011-3467.

19. SOS Approach to Feeding, accessed on October 31, 2020, https://sosapproachtofeeding.com/.

20. Ellyn Satter, "Follow the Division of Responsibility in Feeding," accessed October 31, 2020, https://www.ellynsatterinstitute.org/how-to-feed/the-division-of-responsibility-in-feeding/.

21. Douglas A. Gentile et al., "Protective Effects of Parental Monitoring of Children's Media Use: A Prospective Study," *JAMA Pediatrics* 168, no. 5 (May 2014): 479–84, doi:10.1001/jamapediatrics.2014.146.

BIBLIOGRAPHY

Boyce, W. Thomas. *The Orchid and the Dandelion: Why Some Children Struggle and How All Can Thrive*. New York: Knopf, 2019.

Dictionary.com. "Cooperation." Accessed October 31, 2020. https://www.dictionary.com/browse/cooperation.

Ellyn Satter Institute. "Raise a Healthy Child Who Is a Joy to Feed: Follow the Division of Responsibility in Feeding." Accessed October 31, 2020. https://www.ellynsatterinstitute.org/how-to-feed/the-division-of-responsibility-in-feeding/.

Gentile, Douglas A., R. A. Reimer, A. I. Nathanson, D. A. Walsh, and J. C. Eisenmann. "Protective Effects of Parental Monitoring of Children's Media Use: A Prospective Study." *JAMA Pediatrics* 168, no. 5 (May 2014): 479–84. https://doi.org/10.1001/jamapediatrics.2014.146.

Gradisar, Michael, Kate Jackson, Nicola J. Spurrier, Joyce Gibson, Justine Whitham, Anne Sved Williams, Robyn Dolby, and David J. Kennaway. "Behavioral Interventions for Infant Sleep Problems: A Randomized Controlled Trial." *Pediatrics* 137, no. 6 (June 2016): e20151486. https://doi.org/10.1542/peds.2015-1486.

Hughes, Daniel, Jonathan Baylin, and Daniel J. Siegel. *Brain-Based Parenting: The Neuroscience of Caregiving for Healthy Attachment*. New York: W. W. Norton & Company, Inc., 2012.

Jeon, Hyeonjin, and Seung-Hwan Lee. "From Neurons to Social Beings: Short Review of the Mirror Neuron System Research and Its Socio-Psychological and Psychiatric Implications." *Clinical Psychopharmacology and Neuroscience: The Official Scientific Journal of the Korean College of Neuropsychopharmacology* 16, no. 1 (February 2018): 18–31. https://doi.org/10.9758/cpn.2018.16.1.18.

Kuypers, Leah. "The Zones of Regulation." Accessed October 31, 2020. https://www.zonesofregulation.com/index.html.

Miller, Lucy Jane. *Sensational Kids: Hope and Help for Children with Sensory Processing Disorder*. New York: Penguin Press, 2014.

National Scientific Council on the Developing Child. "Excessive Stress Disrupts the Architecture of the Developing Brain." Accessed October 31, 2020. http://edn.ne.gov/cms/sites/default/files/u1/pdf/se05SE2%20Stress%20 Disrupts%20Architecture%20Dev%20Brain%203.pdf.

Prencipe, Angela, and Phillip David Zelazo. "Development of Affective Decision Making for Self and Other: Evidence for the Integration of First- and Third-Person Perspectives." *Psychological Science* 16, no. 7 (July 2005): 501–5. https://doi.org/10.1111/j.0956-7976.2005.01564.x.

Price, Anna M. H., Melissa Wake, Obioha C. Ukoumunne, and Harriet Hiscock. "Five-Year Follow-Up of Harms and Benefits of Behavioral Infant Sleep Intervention: Randomized Trial." *Pediatrics* 130, no. 4 (October 2012): 643–51. https://doi.org/10.1542/peds.2011-3467.

Rothbart, Mary K., and Brad E. Sheese. "Temperament and Emotion Regulation." In *Handbook of Emotion Regulation*, edited by J. J. Grossion, 331–50. New York: Guildford Press, 2007.

Ruttle, Paula L., Elizabeth A. Shirtcliff, Lisa A. Serbin, Dahlia Ben-Dat Fisher, Dale M. Stack, and Alex E. Schwartzman. "Disentangling Psychobiological Mechanisms Underlying Internalizing and Externalizing Behaviors in Youth: Longitudinal and Concurrent Associations with Cortisol." *Hormones and Behavior* 59, no. 1 (July 2011): 123. https://doi.org/10.1016/j.yhbeh.2010.10.015.

Siegel, Daniel J., and Tina Payne Bryson. *The Whole-Brain Child: 12 Revolutionary Strategies to Nurture Your Child's Developing Mind*. New York: Random House Digital, Inc., 2011.

SOS Approach to Feeding. Accessed on October 31, 2020. https://sos approachtofeeding.com/.

Sowell, Elizabeth R., Paul M. Thompson, Colin J. Holmes, Terry L. Jernigan, and Arthur W. Toga. "*In Vivo* Evidence for Post-Adolescent Brain Maturation in Frontal and Striatal Regions." *Nature Neuroscience* 2, no. 10 (October 1999): 859–61. https://doi.org/10.1038/13154.

INDEX

ABOUT THE AUTHOR

Claire Lerner is a licensed clinical social worker and child development specialist. She served as the director of parenting resources at ZERO TO THREE for more than eighteen years. Claire has also been a practicing clinician for thirty-three years, partnering with parents to do the detective work of decoding their children's behavior to solve their most vexing child-rearing challenges. She also provides training to local preschools and pediatric residents. Claire is the author of hundreds of parenting resources, including books, blogs, podcasts, and videos. She writes a column for PBS Kids, and her work has been published by several parenting publications. She has served as a content expert for numerous national daily newspapers. Claire is the mother of two very spirited children, Sam, 30, and Jess, 28, and two stepchildren, Justin, 30, and Sammy, 27. She lives in Bethesda, Maryland, with her husband, Rich, and two also very spirited pups.